EXERCISE BOOK
to accompany

Rosa/Eschholz

THE WRITER'S BRIEF HANDBOOK
Seventh Edition

Teresa R. Horton
Baker College of Port Huron

Longman

Boston Columbus Indianapolis New York San Francisco Upper Saddle River

Amsterdam Cape Town Dubai London Madrid Milan Munich Paris Montreal Toronto

Delhi Mexico City Sao Paulo Sydney Hong Kong Seoul Singapore Taipei Tokyo

Exercise Book to accompany Rosa/Eschholz, *The Writer's Brief Handbook,* Seventh Edition

Longman is an
imprint of

www.pearsonhighered.com

ISBN 10: 0-205-74408-7
ISBN 13: 978-0-205-74408-4

CONTENTS

iv

A NOTE TO INSTRUCTORS

Thank you for adopting *The Writer's Brief Handbook* and its companion, *Exercise Book* for *The Writer's Brief Handbook*. This exercise book has been designed to help your students practice the many points made in *The Writer's Brief Handbook*. In general, for each rule in the *Handbook*, one or more exercises are presented. Most exercises contain ten problems, and answers for the first five problems are included at the back of this book. A full set of answers is available in a separate publication, entitled the *Answer Key*. Thus, your students can work independently on numbers 1—5, and the remaining problems can be used for homework, quizzes, or as additional practice for students needing help in learning a particular rule or concept.

Format

Each exercise set is explicitly keyed to the rules presented in the *Handbook*; for example, "2c" refers you to the section "Writing the beginning and ending," in Section I, 2 Writing a draft. In order to further help you locate material, a table of contents is also provided.

Instructors who have assigned *The Writer's Brief Handbook* as a textbook may duplicate any or all of these exercises and the answers in the *Answer Key* for distribution to students. The *Exercise Book* may also be purchased by students. In addition, the *Handbook* and the *Exercise Book* are available for purchase as a shrink-wrapped package at a special discount. Instructors interested in additional information on this package discount should call their Pearson Education representative or toll-free 800-852-8024. Or visit our Web site at http://perasonhighered.com to use our Find your rep page.

What is MyCompLab?

 PEARSON

A Pearson English MyLab. Learn more   HOME   LEARN ABOUT   TOURS & TRAINING   SUPPORT

LEARN ABOUT

- What is MyCompLab?
- What's New?
- Success Stories
- Faculty Advocate Program
- Integrating MyCompLab into Your Course
- Meet Our Advisory Board
- Get Involved
- Books Available
- Correlation Guide for Users of the Former Version
- WPA Outcomes Matched to MyCompLab
- MyCompLab for Course Management
- Pearson Tutor Services
- Learn About Other Pearson English MyLabs

What Is MyCompLab?

"Built specifically for writers, MyCompLab is an integrated environment that supports all aspects of the composing process."
– *Stuart Selber, Associate Professor of English and Director of Composition, Penn State University*

view larger   view larger

The new MyCompLab empowers student writers and facilitates writing instruction by uniquely integrating a composing space and ePortfolio with proven resources and tools. In this revolutionary application, students receive feedback within the context of their own writing —encouraging critical thinking and revision while honing their skills based on individual needs. Administrative features developed specifically for writing instruction bring instructors closer to their student writers, make managing assignments and evaluating papers more efficient, and save instructors time.

Taking the market-leading resources for writing, grammar and research that users have come to

How Do Students Register?

"It is easy to get started! Simply follow these easy steps to get into your MyCompLab course."

1 **Find Your Access Code** (it is either packaged with your textbook, or you purchased it separately). You will need this access code and your CLASS ID to log into your MyCompLab course. Your instructor has your CLASS ID number, so make sure you have that before logging in.

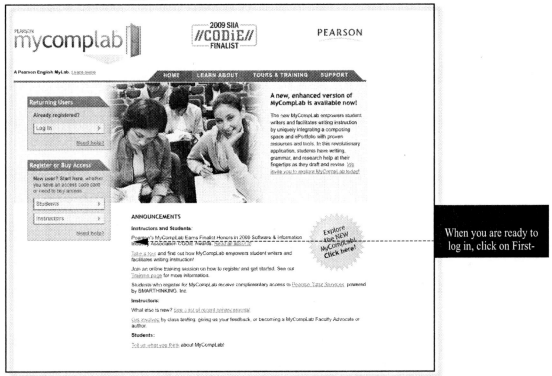

When you are ready to log in, click on First-

2 Click on "Students" under "First-Time Users." Here you will be prompted to enter your access code, enter your e-mail address, and choose your own Login Name and Password. **Once you register, you can click on "Returning Users" and use your new login name and password every time you go back into your course in MyCompLab.**

More on Registering

PEARSON
mycomplab

2009 SIIA
//CODiE//
FINALIST

PEARSON

A Pearson English MyLab. Learn more

HOME | LEARN ABOUT | TOURS & TRAINING | SUPPORT

SUPPORT

▶ Student Support

▶ Instructor Support

▶ Forgot Your Login Info?

▶ System Requirements

Student Support

- Registration Help
- Getting Started
- User Guide
- FAQ Database
- Contact Technical Support

Registration Help

To register for MyCompLab, you need:

- **A student access code** The code is packaged with your textbook or available for purchase on this Web site with a major credit card. (Return to the MyCompLab home page and click **Students** in the "Register or Buy Access" box.) You can also check with your bookstore to purchase a standalone access card. Your unique code will look something like this: SMPLE – FRILL – TONLE – WEIRS · CHOIR – FLEES

- **To register for MyCompLab by redeeming the access card packaged with your textbook, you need:**
  - **A valid email account**(Use an account you'll keep for the duration of your course.)
  - **Your school's ZIP code**

- **To buy access to MyCompLab online, you need:**
  - **A valid email account**(Use an account you'll keep for the duration of your course.)
  - **Your school's ZIP code**
  - **Author, title, edition of your textbook.** You can generally find this information on the first few pages of your book. Ask your instructor if you are not sure.
  - **The version of MyCompLab your instructor is using.** The version is generic or eBook. Ask your instructor if you are not sure. If your instructor is using an eBook, also get the textbook's title and author.

Download a complete guide to registration, login, and getting started with **MyCompLab**.

Still need registration help? Check out our online FAQs.

Resources

MyCompLab provides Resources topics in writing, grammar, and research. These Resources are available to all users of MyCompLab, whether you are working on your own or in an instructor's course.

Each topic includes instructional, multimedia, and/or exercise resources.

- **Instructional resources** define concepts and provide examples of the concept. For some instructional resources, a QuickCheck appears at the end of an instruction. A QuickCheck is one or two questions or examples, and you select the correct answer or example. MyCompLab then displays a pop-up identifying whether your answer is correct or incorrect and why.

  For eBook courses, the instructional resource list also has a link to the relevant section in the eBook.

- **Multimedia resources,** when available, are typically audio clips or videos that reinforce a concept. The multimedia resources include animated and narrated tutorials that range from grammar topics, strategies for developing a draft, guidelines on peer reviews, and tutorials on avoiding plagiarism to deciding on the topic for a paper.

- **Exercises** provide you with the opportunity to practice and apply what you have learned. MyCompLab provides immediate feedback to your answers, letting you know whether your answer is correct or incorrect, which answer is correct, and why that answer is correct. MyCompLab also provides refresher resources to further reinforce the concept. The results of these exercises are logged in your Gradebook's Practice Results.

  Most topics have multiple sets of exercises to provide extensive practice. However, once you complete all the exercises for a topic, MyCompLab displays a **Take Again** link so you have the option of reworking a topic's exercises. The score you get when you retake the exercises replaces the original score.

TIP: A topic's exercises can be recommended by MyCompLab based on the results of a diagnostic assignment or by your instructor when commenting on your writing submissions.

MyCompLab organizes instruction, multimedia, and exercise content by topic. However, you also have access to a Media Index that organizes the content by type (for example, all videos in one list).

I   THE WRITING PROCESS

WRITING PROCESS
1d, f; 2c   **Refer to the Handbook, pp. 4–8, 11–12, 17–21**

Using one of the following suggested topics or an instructor assigned topic, practice using two of the techniques for generating ideas and collecting information: brainstorming, asking questions, clustering, journaling, freewriting, or researching.

Topics:

- healthcare in the U.S.
- job interview skills
- fast-food industry and childhood obesity
- the costs of higher education
- the risks of using a cell phone
- the importance of leadership skills in the workplace

Follow the model in the Handbook in 1d–f and 2c of Section I.

Reflect on which technique worked best for you and that you may use in your writing process.

Now choose one of the topics for which you generated ideas and develop several thesis statements for it. Refer to Section I, 1f. Review the Thesis Essentials on p. 11.

Once you have developed a thesis statement for your topic, write an introduction, using one of the strategies found in 2c of Section I.

Imagine you have completed your essay on the selected topic. Now write a possible concluding paragraph, using one or more of the strategies in 2c of Section I.

WRITING PROCESS

4c, Proofreading   **Refer to the Handbook, pp. 26–27.**

Proofread the writing excerpt that begins on the following page. Mark up the sample essay as you would your own work, making changes on the page. There are 24 errors that need to be corrected.

For example:

> When I travel I always, or at least usually, carry along with me at least teh following items; shaving kit, extra socks, and an extra Fifty Dollars folded inside my shoe. These items has bailed me out of more tight situations then I care to mension.

Answer:

indent 5 spaces

>   wdy
>
> When I travel I always, ~~or at least usually,~~ carry along with me at
>
>   the
>
> least ~~teh~~ following items; shaving kit, extra socks, and an extra Fifty
>
>   d   have
>
> Dollars folded inside my shoe. These items ~~has~~ bailed me out of more
>
>   a   t
>
> tight situations then I care to mension.

"To Much Reality"

Andrea Parker

I have to admit that I am one of the count less American's sucked into the drama of realty television programs, such as Foxs "Joe Millionaire" and "The Bachelor." But after several years of mindlessly watching other people experience their life. I'm feeling bored and unchallenged, and even a little insulted. I find myself aimlessly flipping through the channels, I am longing for a good drama or situation comedy. The problem is, while I've moved on, most network programming has'nt. The reason is simple Networks are raking in big profits from reality television.

First the cost of production reality television is considerably less than many other types of programming. Consider the fact that reality TV stars start off as unknowns, with little clout to command high salaries. For example, contestints from the reality show "Big Brother" earn only $750.00 per week, and participints on "American Idol" and "The Bachelor" are not paid a salary at all. Compare that to the highpriced salaries of television actor from the show "To and a Half Men," who makes a reported $860,000 per episode Charlie Sheen. Another cost saving measure are the fact that networks do not need to pay for sets or scripts. When Jo Frost from "Super Nanny" steps into a familys life to provide guidance on child rearing, the set is the familys actual home, and because the script is written from the "mouths of babes," it costes no thing to produce.

the second reason reality television is so profitable is that...

3

WRITING ARGUMENTATIVE ESSAYS

4, Distinguishing between Fact and Opinion   **Refer to the Handbook, pp. 56–64.**

Directions: Identify which of the following statements are fact and which are opinion. (F or O)

1. _____   Higher taxes are not acceptable.

2. _____   A Democrat should win the next presidential election.

3. _____   Some people have a life-threatening allergy to peanuts.

4. _____   Studying history is not relevant to today's workplace.

5. _____   The legal drinking age in most states is twenty-one.

6. _____   Spending money to explore Mars is useless.

7. _____   In 2009 Barack Obama was elected the first African American president.

8. _____   The most important part of getting a job is creating a strong resume.

9. _____   Attending college increases a person's earning potential for a lifetime.

10. _____   Exercise has been proven to lower the risk of heart disease.

WRITING ARGUMENTATIVE ESSAYS

4a, Facts versus Claims   **Refer to the Handbook, pp. 56–57.**

Identify each of the following statements as either a fact or a claim. If the statement is a fact, rewrite it to make the statement into a claim. If the statement is already a claim, simply label it as such.

Example:

(   ) In 2009 OSHA guidelines recommend that all healthcare workers be vaccinated for the H1N1 virus.

In the example above, first identify the statement as a fact. Then, rewrite the sentence and convert it into a claim. One possible answer might look like this:

(fact   ) In 2009 OSHA guidelines recommended that all healthcare workers be vaccinated for the H1N1 virus.

(claim   ) In 2009 OSHA took steps to protect healthcare workers from the H1N1 virus.

1. (   ) Every American citizen has the right to vote.

   (   )

2. (   ) Some animal rights advocates object to the use of animals for medical research and testing.

   (   )

3. (   ) The obesity rate among children in the U.S. has been steadily growing over the past two decades.

   (   )

4. (   ) Paintball should be an Olympic medal sport.

   (   )

5. (   ) Thomas Jefferson signed the Declaration of Independence on July 4, 1776.

   (   )

6. (   ) *Avatar* was the most expensive movie ever made.

   (   )

7. (   ) Global warming has created the conditions responsible for El Niño.

   (   )

8. (   ) U.S. Department of Transportation studies have revealed that in collisions
                 between cars and trucks/sport utility vehicles, 80% of the fatalities occur in the
                 cars.

   (   )

9. (   ) College is a good investment for students studying business.

   (   )

10. (   ) Though 30% of all cancers are associated with tobacco use, the government
                  has not made it an illegal substance.

    (   )

WRITING ARGUMENTATIVE ESSAYS

4b, Logical Appeals   **Refer to the Handbook, pp. 59–60.**

For each of the following sentences, identify the corresponding logical fallacy.

Example: Either you are part of the problem or part of the solution.

Answer: **Either/Or Thinking**

1. If every family would just recycle its household waste, we wouldn't need to worry about excessive landfills.

2. If you vote, then you are a patriot.

3. The governments of Russia and China are similar because they are near each other.

4. If you really cared about yourself, you would lose weight and lower your blood pressure.

5. If the president can afford to send troops around the world, we ought to be able to find a solution to homelessness.

6. My brother and several cousins lost weight on the Atkins diet, so everyone who wants to lose weight should try it.

7. Every time my mother-in-law visits, it rains and I get a cold; therefore, I believe my mother-in-law brings bad luck.

8. She would not be a good Girl Scout leader because she doesn't even have a daughter.

9. The older generation does not care about the national debt. It is the younger generation that will have to pay the bill some day.

10. If you can't get an A in a class, there's no sense continuing with school.

A sample e-mail from a student to a professor appears below. The message contains twelve violations of the guidelines in Section II, 5a. Name each of the errors in the spaces provided.

TO: <u>pjones@stateuniversity.edu</u>

FROM: <u>tkelly@stateuniversity.edu</u>

DATE/TIME: 20FEB2010; 21:17:12

SUBJ:

Dear Prof. Jones,

I hope u get this bfore class. FYI, I will not be in class this week. I need to stay w/ my aunt b/c she just had knee surgery and cannot be left alone☹. I'M SORRY. I need to get this wek's assignments ASAP. Plz get back to me right away.

Kel

---

1. _____

2. _____

3. _____

4. _____

5. _____

6. _____

7. _____

8. _____

9. _____

10. _____

11. _____

12. _____

9

7a, Formatting a Business Letter   **Refer to the Handbook, pp. 75-79.**

In the following sample business letter by an author submitting a manuscript to a publisher, correct the formatting errors for each of the numbered locations. The first one is done for you as an example.

In addition, there are twelve formatting flaws in this sample page; list them and describe what should have been done instead. Use the spaces provided.

   (a) <u>top of page</u> to <u>top of return address</u>: 6–12 line spaces (use this variation to balance the letter visually on the page from top to bottom)

1. **(b)** line spacing:

2. **(c)** left margin:

3. **(d)** bottom margin:

4. **(e)** right margin:

5. appropriate letter type (full block; modified block; indented)?

6. _____

7. _____

8. _____

9. _____

10. _____

11. _____

12. _____

(1)

2112 West Street

Port Huron, Mich **(5)** 48041

(2)

February 16, 2010

Ms. Sharon Nelson

(6) Editor, **(7)** Main Headquarters

Preston Publishing, Inc.

Memphis, Michigan 48041

Dear Ms. Nelson, **(8)**

(3)   I am submitting the enclosed manuscript for my children's book titled *All Good Monkeys* for your consideration. I regard Preston Publishing as the most respected publisher of children's books, and I would appreciate any feedback you might give me concerning this manuscript.

(4)   I believe *All Good Monkeys* has an engaging and educational plot that appeals to both children and teachers. And the topic of "global and cultural awareness" could not be timelier. I look forward to hearing your ideas about this manuscript. **(9)**

Sincerely Yours **(10)** **(11)**

Cammy Davis

Enclosure Manuscript **(12)**

III   PARAGRAPHS

PARAGRAPHS

1, Unity   **Refer to the Handbook, pp. 85–89.**

Examine each of the following sample paragraphs for unity. First underline the topic sentence of each paragraph. Then cross out any words, phrases, or clauses in the paragraph that do not develop the topic sentence.

For example:

> The modern field spaniel satisfies the eye of the serious show dog fancier who appreciates his physical beauty. Best described as moderate and well-balanced with no exaggerated features, the field spaniel is known for his beautiful head. Framed by low-set and well-feathered long ears that lay close to the sculpted skull, the head of the field spaniel at once conveys the impression of nobility, intelligence and good nature. Field spaniels are expensive and may cost up to two thousand dollars.

Answer:

> <u>The modern field spaniel satisfies the eye of the serious show dog fancier who appreciates his physical beauty.</u> Best described as moderate and well-balanced with no exaggerated features, the field spaniel is known for his beautiful head. Framed by low-set and well-feathered long ears that lay close to the sculpted skull, the head of a field spaniel at once conveys the impression of nobility, intelligence and good nature. ~~Field spaniels are expensive and may cost up to two thousand dollars.~~

> —modified from Becky Jo Wolkenheim, *Field Spaniel*

1. Critters other than bears are far more likely to inflict mayhem on your camp. Raccoons, skunks, ring-tailed cats, pack rats, mice, though often adorable, and other nighttime invaders are all far more real threats. You will want to dress warm because the temperature can drop dramatically at night. For the most part, the same measures you take against bears will work with other animals. In some established sites, mice can be a real problem. In mouse country try hanging the food bag from the rafter, with a can lid placed halfway down the cord.

> —modified from Alan S. Kesselheim, *Canoeing in the Wilderness*

2. In April General McClellan finally moved his Army of the Potomac against the enemy. The Potomac is a beautiful river. Striking south by way of the peninsula between the James and York rivers, he prepared to attack Yorktown. The Confederates allowed McClellan to complete his careful, lengthy preparations for the assault, and evacuated the fortress without firing a shot. McClellan then moved in a complicated series of forays. All of McClellan's maneuvers only succeeded in giving President Lincoln, who was married to Mary Todd Lincoln, the idea that he was trying to win the war by tactics rather than by fighting.

   —modified from Keith Jennison, *The Humorous Mr. Lincoln*

3. "Sticks and stones can break my bones, but words can never hurt me." This popular children's chant could not be more wrong, and it is a good example of an idiom. Words may not literally break people's bones, but they can leave psychological scars as surely as stones can leave physical scars. I have a scar on my arm from a stone. As one writer explains, "Our identities, who and what we are, how others see us, are greatly affected by the names we are called and the words with which we are labeled." This is why almost all communication ethicists warn public speakers to avoid name-calling and other forms of abusive language.

   —modified from Stephen Lucas, *The Art of Public Speaking*

4. To avoid damage to specimens, they should be stored in individual trays or boxes. Each specimen should be individually wrapped in newspaper or other protective material to prevent chipping or scratching, as this will add protection. Crystal groups are usually very fragile and should be packed in tubes or boxes with suitable wrapping and carried in special collecting bags. My favorite rocks are quartz crystals. Because rock and mineral specimens are so valuable, every precaution should be taken when transporting them to a new location so they are not damaged.

   —modified from Dr. R.F. Symes, *Rocks and Minerals*

5. I had many reasons for wanting to leave the ship *Saint Anna.* Our journey had been dogged by misfortune from the very start. The ship was built in 1898. Serious illness, a pervasive doubt that our fortunes would soon change, the certainty that we were at the mercy of hostile natural forces, and finally, the growing concern about our inadequate food supply, were grounds for all manner of disagreements and flaring tempers. And we were convinced that the *Saint Anna* would never free herself from the ice.

   —modified from Valerian Albanov, *In the Land of White Death*

6. Trappers slogged through the frigid streams and ponds, which were really quite beautiful, of every valley in beaver country, searching for the telltale dams and lodges built by their quarry. Once the beaver's daily routes from lodge to dam or logging site were determined, traps could be set along the way to intercept the unsuspecting animal on its way to work. More often tappers would submerge a trap underwater, anchoring it with a stake. The trap was then baited with a twig, left protruding above the water, which was sprinkled with the beaver's own secretion, enhanced with cloves, cinnamon, and other exotic ingredients. Beavers are large brown furry rodents with small eyes, small rounded ears, large orange teeth, and a large flat, scaly tail. Catching an animal as clever as the beaver was not a simple task.

   —modified from Arthur King Peters, *Seven Trails West*

7. The best place (but not the only place) to start your entry garden is right around the front door. By starting there rather than planting broad beds along the length of your entry path or at the driveway end of your path, you will feel more comfortable as you tackle this more manageable space. Once you get the garden around the door established, you can build out from there in a series of comfortable stages, each of which can be made to feel complete. For example, you may create an entry path, planting flowers close to where people walk so they brush against the fragrant leaves or flowers to release aroma. Vegetables should be planted in the backyard.

   —modified from Gordon Hayward, *The Welcoming Garden*

8. The concept of trends in jewelry style is nothing new. For thousands of years humans have adorned themselves with jewelry, and for most of those years the styles were fairly consistent within societies. Household tools such as wire cutters and round-nosed pliers can be used to make jewelry. In the Viking culture, for example, leaders wore gold and silver armbands, collars, and chains, while commoners wore clay, glass, and amber beads. Just a few decades ago, solid metal chains were all the rage (though there were certainly other popular items as well) in this country and others. Today the emphasis is on unique, eye-catching, free styles that suit the wearer. History shows that early people and people today share a common love for jewelry.

   —modified from Dawn Cusick, *Making Bead and Wire Jewelry*

9. Nouns are, by definition, "people, place, and thing" words. It is easy to see that objects are nouns—things such as pencils, televisions, your great-aunt Lula. But abstract things such as qualities and ideas can be nouns too—*love* is a noun, and *egotism* is a noun, and *spoilage.* Many people struggle with writing because they do not understand grammar. Nouns can be singular, when you are talking about one thing (*box*) and nouns can be plural, when you're talking about more than one thing (*boxes*). Adjectives are descriptive words, such as *gorgeous*, *hideous*, *smelly*, or *baggy*.

   —modified from The Princeton Review, *Grammar Smart: A Guide to Perfect Usage*

10. There are two types of fibers used to make rope. Even early cave dwellers used ropes. Vegetable fibers are short and must be spun and twisted to create the long yarns and strands needed for rope. It is the countless fiber ends that give traditional ropes their characteristic hairy appearance and useful surface grip (and sometimes surface grip is important). Long synthetic filaments, however, run the full length of the rope they form, so the manmade cordage is smooth—unless filaments are purposely chopped into shorter lengths of staple fibers to make ropes that recapture the desirable handling qualities of the older natural cordage. Ropes can be made to make jewelry or beautiful macramé artwork.

   —modified from Geoffrey Budworth, *The Ultimate Encyclopedia* of *Knots & Ropework*

PARAGRAPHS

2b, Development Strategies 1   Refer to the Handbook, pp. 90-95.

There are many methods of developing and organizing information, both within paragraphs and the essay as a whole. For example:

Narration: telling a story, most often relating events in chronological order.

Description: describing scenes, most often ordering the items spatially, as a movie camera might capture a scene.

Examples and illustration: citing examples.

Facts, statistics, reasons: using factual information, including numerical summaries.

Definition: providing an extended definition.

Process analysis: explaining a procedure, usually in a step-by-step description.

Comparison and contrast: comparing two things (demonstrating their similarities) and/or contrasting things (demonstrating their dissimilarities).

Analogy: comparing a complex or unfamiliar subject to another topic typically more widely known and understood.

Classification: grouping topics into larger classes on the basis of one or more criteria that demonstrate shared similarities.

Cause and effect: explaining the causal link between two or more subjects.

Mixed strategies: employing more than one of the preceding strategies. Many of the paragraphs in the preceding exercise use mixed strategies.

Referring to the sample paragraphs on pages 12–15, list the development strategy(ies) you think the author uses.

For example: Becky Jo Wolkenheim, *Field Spaniel*

Answer: <u>description</u>

1. Alan S. Kesselheim, *Canoeing in the Wilderness:*

   _____

2. Keith Jennison, *The Humorous Mr. Lincoln:*

   _____

3. Stephen Lucas, *The Art of Public Speaking:*

_____

4. Dr. R.F. Symes, *Rocks and Minerals:*

_____

5. Valerian Albanov, *In the Land of White Death:*

_____

6. Arthur King Peters, *Seven Trails West:*

_____

7. Gordon Hayward, *The Welcoming Garden:*

_____

8. Dawn Cusick, *Making Bead and Wire Jewelry:*

_____

9. The Princeton Review, *Grammar Smart: A Guide to Perfect Usage:*

_____

10. Geoffrey Budworth, *The Ultimate Encyclopedia* of *Knots & Ropework*

_____

PARAGRAPHS

2b, Development Strategies 2   **Refer to the Handbook, pp. 90-95.**

For each writing assignment listed here, provide one or more development strategies that you could successfully employ to write on that topic. (If necessary, refer to the list of development strategies on pages 15–16.)

For example: Explain the concept of separation of power within the U.S. government.

Answer: definition; illustration

1. Explain how the structure of family life has changed in the last decade.

2. Discuss the importance of a college education today.

3. Explain the slower-than-expected adoption of recycling.

4. Compare your life to a well-known children's story.

5. Describe the qualities that make a great leader.

6. Describe the differences between attending college as an 18-year-old and returning to school as an adult.

7. Explain what a family means to you.

8. What is your definition of happiness?

9. Explain what you believe to be the most challenging problems facing the United States today and why.

10. Describe how to change the oil in a car.

PARAGRAPHS

3, Coherence   **Refer to the Handbook, pp. 96–101.**

Writers use four principal tools to make their writing coherent: organization, transitions, repetition of key words and phrases, and parallel structures.

After reading the following passage complete the exercises that follow it.

When I stepped out into the bright sunlight from the darkness of the movie house, I had only two things on my mind: Paul Newman and a ride home. I went on walking home, thinking about the movie, and then suddenly I had some company. Greasers like me can't walk alone too much or we get jumped by the Socs. I was only two blocks from home then, so I started walking a little faster.

I knew it wasn't any use though—the fast walking, I mean—even before the Corvair pulled up beside me and five Socs got out. I was sweating something fierce, although I was cold. I glanced around for a pop bottle-but there was nothing. So I stood there like a bump on a log while they surrounded me.

"Hey, grease," one said in an over-friendly voice. One of them laughed, then cussed me out in a low voice. I couldn't think of anything to say. There just isn't a whole lot you can say while waiting to get mugged, so I kept my mouth shut. "Need a haircut, greaser?" The medium-sized blond pulled a knife out of his back pocket and flipped the blade open.

I finally thought of something to say. "No." I was backing up, away from that knife. Of course I backed right into one of them. They had me down in a second. They had my arms and legs pinned down and one of them was sitting on my chest with his knees on my elbows, and if you don't think that hurts, you're crazy. I fought to get loose, and almost did for a second; then they tightened up on me and the one on my chest slugged me a couple of times. So I lay still, swearing at them between gasps. A blade was held against my throat.

"How'd you like that haircut to begin just below the chin?"

Then there were shouts and the pounding of feet, and the Socs jumped up and left me lying there, gasping. As I lay there, I wondered what in the world was happening—people were jumping over me and running by me and I was too dazed to figure it out. Then someone had me under the armpits and was hauling me to my feet. It was Darry.

"Are you all right, Ponyboy?"

—S.E. Hinton, *The Outsiders*

18

1. How is the sample passage organized? (Chronologically? Spatially? Logically?) Explain your choice.

2. Underline the transitional words and phrases in the story. How do they relate to the type of organization used by the author?

For Section III, 4. regarding additional examples of beginning and ending paragraphs, refer to Section I, The Writing Process, 2, Writing a Draft, Part C, Writing the Beginning and Ending.

STYLE

1, Parallelism   **Refer to the Handbook, pp. 103–104.**

Rewrite the following sentences to improve their parallel structure.

For example: We serve hamburgers and hot dogs on the weekends and Italian sausage too.

Correction: **We serve hamburgers, hot dogs, and Italian sausage on the weekends.**

1. I will be making brownies and cookies for the bake sale, and I also want to make a chocolate cake.

2. When I am in Florida I enjoy spending time snorkeling, diving, and I collect sea shells too.

3. The obesity epidemic is mainly due to the rise of fast-food restaurants, the poor quality of school lunches, and children are inactive because they are watching too much television and playing video games.

4. I hired Joe to build my new kitchen because he is an excellent carpenter and I find that I can trust him.

5. As the deer grazed in the field, the birds were eating from the bird feeder.

6. Our team is well prepared and has great equipment; our coach too is excellent, and we've had a lot of practices.

7. Not only is he a nice man, but he is visiting his mother in the nursing home.

8. The boy decided not to go to school, but swimming in the river.

9. Is it better to stand fast on environmental policy than having a compromise in order to save jobs?

10. At the local drug store she works as the manager, and she delivered medication to the elderly customers.

STYLE

Rewrite the following sentences to eliminate the misplaced and dangling modifiers.

For example: Kathy caught a fish wearing a pink and white bathing suit.

Correction: Wearing a pink and white bathing suit, Kathy caught a fish.

1. Dipped in ketchup, John ate the french fries.

2. Threatened with extinction, the EPA wrote new rules for the spotted owl.

3. The man walked the dog in a black leather jacket.

4. Young and inexperienced jobs were few and far between, Jim discovered.

5. I wrote directions for my friend to the house.

6. Blazing with every primary color, Kelsie held the African parrot on her arm.

7. I saw a big fish with my mask and snorkel on.

8. It was so cold that I walked my dog Belle dressed in snow boots, a winter parka, and fur-lined gloves.

9. I gave Della a book in the library written by Faulkner.

10. I saw the Golden Gate Bridge riding my bike over the hill.

Correct the inappropriate shifts in person or number in the following sentences. Indicate the type of shift you are correcting.

For example: My brother joined the Navy. They offer many educational opportunities.

Correction: **My brother joined the Navy. It offers many educational opportunities. (number)**

1. The Farmer's Organization has grown to over 3 million members in the past 2 years, and they are very happy about the added revenue.

2. Every child should keep his lunch and backpack in their locker.

3. If students who wish to order a yearbook, he or she will want to order early.

4. My father worked for forty-two years at General Motors; they made him retire last month.

5. If a person wants to fly on a commercial airline, they should be aware there is a forty-dollar charge for each carry-on item.

6. Although one prepared for the storm, I was nonetheless scared by its strength.

7. We were told by the tour guide that you can take pictures inside the cathedrals.

8. Denise reminded us to be sure to come early so they could get a good seat.

9. When I asked Nelson about the Baseball Hall of Fame, he said that they are located in Cooperstown, NY.

10. The Navy has a new recruiting slogan because they want to attract the best men.

3b, Shifts 2   **Refer to the Handbook, pp. 107.**

Correct the inappropriate shifts in verb tense.

For example: The dog sniffed the bushes in the back yard and smells a bunny.

Correction: **The dog sniffed around the bushes in the backyard and smelled a bunny.**

1. The students in Ms. Archer's English class write essays and performed the play *Romeo and Juliet.*

2. At the surprise party, the cars were parked on another street, the lights were turned off, and music was playing softly in the background.

3. Tomorrow we will walk to school but rode the bus home.

4. The Olympic skaters warmed up before their performance, and practice their most difficult moves.

5. While Harry was on vacation in Ireland, a robber breaks into his home.

6. I will not have time to make dinner before my meeting, so I will be bringing home pizza from the party store.

7. The clerk questioned why I want to return the black dress.

8. The cocker spaniel eats her food quickly before the big dogs have eaten.

9. The interviewer asks interesting questions as soon as the celebrity has taken her seat.

10. If we pay for the trip in advance, we will be saving over two hundred dollars per person.

Correct the inappropriate shifts in subject or voice. Indicate the type of shift you are correcting.

For example: We noticed the hurricane damage as the town was approached.

Correction: **We noticed the hurricane damage as we approached the town. (subject)**

1. Screaming, the rollercoaster dropped over sixty feet in thirty seconds.

2. The donuts were enjoyed by everyone, and then we all warmed up by the fire.

3. Dancing in the pouring rain, my new hat began to wilt.

4. Broken into a million pieces, my aunt Charlene swept up the remnants of the broken vase.

5. We chose to order the chilidogs because they were buy one get one free. Sharing the french fries also saved us money too.

6. When our flight landed in Miami, dinner was our first thought.

7. The gift of cooking passed us by, but I still enjoy making a meal for company.

8. Jumping over the puddle, the cake slipped from the plate and landed on the sidewalk.

9. The idea of raising taxes was approached as Congress searched for ways to pay for the healthcare bill.

10. If someone wants to learn to read faster and better, it can be done through practice.

STYLE

Edit the following sentences to eliminate irrelevant detail.

For example: The author's second novel, nearly four hundred pages long, did not receive the widespread acclaim of her first.

Correction: **The author's second novel did not receive the widespread acclaim of her first.**

1. Most spaniels are kept to be indoor companions and not hunters, which is, I personally think, the best place for them.

2. Charles Dickens, who died in 1870, was a prolific author, working on up to three novels at the same time.

3. Over the last decade, the cost of oil has almost doubled, not to mention the price of groceries, taking up more of Americans' disposable income.

4. During our summer vacation, which turned out to be quite cold, Joe proposed to Lisa.

5. The interstate highway system, originally constructed for reasons of national security, is now badly in need of extensive rebuilding.

6. We should all be careful of credit cards, which we really don't need, because there can be many hidden fees and excessive interest rates.

7. The area between the Ohio and Mississippi rivers, home many years ago to Native Americans, once was known as the West.

8. Staffed by trained personal in airport security, the Northwest terminal moves travelers quickly through the security check.

9. President Obama, who is happily married, gave his first State of the Union Address on January 27, 2010.

10. When I tasted Pauline's pecan pie, which I'm sure was over my daily calorie limit, I knew that her recipe would win first place at this year's county fair.

4b, Mixed or Illogical Constructions   **Refer to the Handbook, pp. 110–111.**

Edit the following sentences to eliminate mixed or illogical constructions.

For example: The Golden Eagle award has prestige, and it is an honor for Joe to receive it.

Correction: Joe was honored to receive the prestigious Golden Eagle award.

   1. Congressman Jones said that the new spending bill won't increase nobody's taxes.

   2. A bait and switch is where a company advertises a product at a very low price to bring in customers, but does not actually have enough of that product on hand.

   3. The baker made a triple chocolate cake; however, they forgot to add baking powder.

   4. We were skiing down the north side of the mountain, when we sailed into a clump of evergreens.

   5. Can you borrow me the new Stephen King book you just finished reading?

   6. The salary for becoming a census taker is expensive.

   7. The master gardener planted two perennial gardens that was designed to bloom from early spring through fall.

   8. Martin Luther King Jr., his speeches powerful, always captured the attention of his audiences.

   9. Even though he won the election by a landslide, Mayor Timlin can't seem to do nothing right this year.

   10. The Johnstown's flood of 1881 was because the South Fork Dam failed, and Americans wake to the devastating news that over two thousand people have perished.

5a, Subordination—Choppy Sentences   **Refer to the Handbook, pp. 112–113.**

Using subordination, rewrite each set of short sentences as one sentence.

For example: We planted corn for 8 hours. We were very tired. We went to the fair that night.

Rewritten: **Although we planted corn for 8 hours and we were very tired, we still went to the fair that night.**

1. Let the yeast and liquids rise in the bowl. Add the flour. Knead the dough and add flour until it no longer sticks to your fingers.

2. I read the quote for the new family room. The quote was out of my price range. We will put off adding the new addition until next year.

3. Our university library has over one million volumes. It covers most areas of information in depth. It also has information that is up-to-date. I do most of my research there.

4. I am trying to lose weight. I am eating salads every day. I am not sure if I can lose two dress sizes by our summer vacation.

5. The Statue of Liberty once again looks beautiful. It was a gift from the French people. It was dedicated in 1886. It was restored for its centennial. It is more than one hundred years old.

6. My book club meets once a month. We take turns choosing the book. Everyone brings a snack to share.

7. Luke studied all weekend for the exam. He was tired. He did well on the exam on Monday.

8. The staff meeting was very tense. Our boss was angry with our poor quarterly performance. I went home with a headache.

9. My mother is a Stones' fan. My father is a Beatles' fan. They are both diehards. They still argue over which group is better. I have to listen to these childish discussions.

10. Our soccer team is small. The players are inexperienced Many players are out sick this week. I think our team will lose the game tonight.

5c, Coordination—Ideas of Equal Importance   **Refer to the Handbook, pp. 113.**

Using coordination, rewrite each set of short sentences as one sentence.

For example: Working with killer whales can be dangerous. Handlers should be well trained.

Rewritten: **Working with killer whales can be dangerous, so handlers should be well trained.**

1. I had not eaten for seven hours. I ate an entire pizza when I finally got home.

2. I believe that he is guilty of stealing the other students' lunches. I believe there are extenuating circumstances.

3. My great-uncle does not smoke. He also does not drink.

4. Joes is a star athlete on the baseball and football teams. He plays the violin in the orchestra.

5. This rain is good for people. It is filling the reservoirs.

6. My cousin does not want a formal and expensive wedding. My sister does not want a formal and expensive wedding.

7. I use sunscreen on my face and wear a hat every day. I have wrinkles around my eyes and small brown age spots on my face.

8. I usually enjoy Martin Scorsese movies. His movies are dark and quirky and at times, hilarious. I did not like *Shutter Island.*

9. I can take the 7:10 train. I can catch the 7:20 bus.

10. Peoples of the ancient cultures of Mexico discovered the delectable power of chocolate. People around the world are eternally grateful.

6b, Logical Order   **Refer to the Handbook, pp. 114.**

Rewrite each of the following sentences to improve its logical and/or climactic sequence.

For example: Our team won the bicycle race, trained for eight weeks, and monitored our diets closely.

Rewritten: Our team trained for eight weeks, monitored our diets closely, and won the bicycle race.

1. Glen Close won an Oscar, arrived in a silver gown by Oscar de la Renta, and danced at an exclusive party until six in the morning.

2. Bonds had a terrible day when we were at the ball park; he struck out in the first, seventh, and fifth innings.

3. I like a movie if it has a good story, ends happily, and begins well.

4. After Kelly delivered her baby, she was in labor for six hours and we counted the baby's toes.

5. I saw the paint had been restored and the back had several deep scratches and then I examined the antique.

6. After he pulled out of the parking lot, John drove home, ate a hamburger and fries, and went through the drive-through.

7. The ground thaws, winter snow melts into the ground, and the daffodils begin to sprout.

8. To pay your monthly bills, first write the checks, then deposit the money in your account, and then figure which bills to pay.

9. John began his research paper by reading on his topic, taking notes, and finding a topic.

10. Before I work out, I stretch my muscles, warm up with some soft music, and get out of my work clothes.

6c, Active Voice   **Refer to the Handbook, pp. 114–115.**

Rewrite the following sentences to change the active voice to the passive voice or vice versa.

For example: The Detroit Institute of Arts is well-loved by me. (passive voice)

Rewritten: **I love the Detroit Institute of Arts.** (active voice)

 1. The decorations, balloons, food, and even the cake were bought by grandma.

 2. The deep gash on Don's face was stitched by the plastic surgeon.

 3. The teenager was given a speeding ticket by the county sheriff.

 4. The kite was pushed by the wind into the power lines.

 5. I was given an ultimatum by my boss as soon as I returned from Phoenix.

 6. "The Star-Spangled Banner" was sung by Karen at the opening game of the Detroit Red
    Wings.

 7. Many immigrants were examined by the U.S. Naturalization Service at Ellis Island.

 8. The boy was taught his good manners by his maternal grandmother.

 9. The family dog is antagonized by the boy every day.

10. Kayla's cornbread and cranberry stuffing was praised by all the women in her family.

7a, Sentence Variety 1   **Refer to the Handbook, pp. 116–118.**

Rewrite the following sentences to eliminate the overuse of short, simple sentences.

For example: Honeybees are familiar insects. Honeybees have a bright color pattern to warn predators. They have a weapon to defend themselves.

Rewritten: Honeybees are familiar insects that have bright color patterns to warn predators that they have a weapon to defend themselves.

1. The farm workers labored in the fields all day. They quickly ate all the sandwiches and salad we gave them.

2. Don and Susan are young. They are a nice couple. They are too young to get married.

3. Hurricane Katrina devastated New Orleans. It also devastated most of the Gulf Coast. People from around the country worked together to ease the suffering of those who were affected.

4. Fly over any major U.S. city. Look out the plane's window. You will be shocked by the number of swimming pools you will see.

5. Accounting can be a very difficult class. Many students fail accounting class. John got an "A" in accounting.

6. There are many reasons people change jobs. They want to make more money. They want to seek a challenge. They want to fit in better with their co-workers.

7. I heard Lazlo's newest album on the radio. It's another hit, I think.

8. In the morning I wake up the kids for school. I take a shower and dress. I pack lunches. I feed the dogs.

9. I read through the recipes in my new *Taste of Home* book. The pictures looked delicious. I felt hungry.

10. Congress proposed a new tax hike. It raised many questions. One of them was whom would it benefit.

7b, Sentence Variety 2   **Refer to the Handbook, pp. 118.**

Rewrite sentences A and B to begin with the structure indicated.

Given: Each piece of Norman Rockwell's art captures a bit of American history and displays the beauty and simplicity of everyday life.

Begin with an infinitive: To capture a bit of American history, each piece of Norman Rockwell's art displays the beauty and simplicity of everyday life.

Begin with a participle: Capturing a bit of American history, each piece of Norman Rockwell's art displays the beauty and simplicity of everyday life.

Begin with a subordinate clause: Because Norman Rockwell wants to capture a bit of American history, each piece of his art displays the beauty and simplicity of everyday life.

Begin with a prepositional phrase: In each piece of his art, Norman Rockwell captures a bit of American history and displays the beauty and simplicity of everyday life.

A. I planted the dahlia bulbs indoors in January and watered them every day so they would be ready to plant outside in the spring.

1. *Begin with an infinitive*:

2. *Begin with a participle*:

3. *Begin with a subordinate clause*:

4. *Begin with a prepositional phrase*:

B: In 1789 French revolutionaries began a *Reign of Terror* to crush those who did not support the revolution.

5. *Begin with an infinitive*:

6. *Begin with a participle:*

7. *Begin with a subordinate clause:*

8. *Begin with a prepositional phrase*:

V   WORD CHOICE

1, Eliminating Clutter   **Refer to the Handbook, pp. 121–125.**

Rewrite each of the following wordy sentences to make them concise and direct.

Example: The police officers roped off the crime scene, as they usually do, and the neighbors had to watch from a distance.

Rewritten: The police officers roped off the crime scene, and the neighbors had to watch from a distance.

1. The famous actor, although, perhaps not incredibly famous, asked for a seat in the back of the restaurant so he would not be bothered by his fans.

2. Kelly was the only person alone in the office Wednesday night, though this was unusual for a Wednesday night, so she must be the one who stole the money from the cash box.

3. The children were told, as they were often told, that sending text messages during dinner was rude.

4. The musicians, which seem to me obviously hadn't practiced enough, couldn't even play the national anthem without mistakes.

5. Can you explain why it is that schools of fish, which live in the water, and flocks of birds that fly in the air, move as a single group with similar coordinated motions?

6. People in the midwestern states experienced more snow this year, with higher snowfall totals, than they have witnessed in the past two decades.

7. The teacher took a cut in pay that reduced her salary.

8. The construction worker, who did manual labor, was worn down by a lifetime of hard work.

9. While everyone's point of view, and ideas, and feelings must be taken into account and assessed carefully and thoughtfully, it seems to me that in the end the president is kind of charged with the task of leading rather than evaluating.

10. Ronald Reagan, for all intents and purposes, worked hard to reduce the people's dependence on the Federal Government.

WORDS

2c, General versus Specific Words   Refer to the Handbook, pp. 126–127.

For each general word in the list, provide a specific example.

Example: exercise: **jogging**

  1.   books:

  2.   animals:

  3.   ice cream:

  4.   governments:

  5.   holidays:

  6.   colors:

  7.   relatives:

  8.   dances:

  9.   music:

10.   bugs:

35

2c, Abstract versus Concrete Words   **Refer to the Handbook, pp. 126–127.**

Identify each word in the following list as either abstract or concrete.

Example: emotions: abstract

1.   brilliant:

2.   trophy:

3.   test:

4.   purple:

5.   stars:

6.   book:

7.   weak:

8.   apple:

9.   truth:

10. pencil:

11. honesty:

12. bright:

13. delirious:

14. puzzle:

15. tall:

16. rusty:

17. slippery:

18. water:

19. music:

20. arrogance:

2d, Idioms   **Refer to the Handbook, pp. 127.**

Correct the misuse of prepositions in the following sentences containing idiomatic expressions.

Example: We will stop by the store on the way home.

Correction: **We will stop at the store on the way home.**

1.   The mother rewarded the boy by a chocolate ice cream cone.

2.   Kelly arrived early at the bookstore so that she would be sure and get an autograph.

3.   Please use the tool in the purpose that it was intended.

4.   Brick is superior than wood when building a house in this part of the country.

5.   I want to work and improve my jump shot for the next game.

6.   Their delivery route was different than ours.

7.   The Republicans are angry at the Democrats' resolution.

8.   Fifth Avenue runs parallel with Walton Street.

9.   I found my way home in the dark by a flashlight.

10.   We are ecstatic by the way the new office is decorated.

3a-e, Appropriate Formality   **Refer to the Handbook, pp. 129–132.**

Rewrite each of the following sentences, substituting the italicized word or phrase with a more formal expression.

Example: I *flew out* of the office to make it to David's soccer game.

Answer: I rushed out of the office to make it to David's soccer game.

1.   There are so many *things* I have to do before the wedding.

2.   The new Danielle Steele book is *really awesome*.

3.   You will need to *step on it* if you want to arrive at the theater before the movie starts.

4.   Collecting stamps was Phil's *thing*.

5.   Janet was *bummed* that Paul did not call her back for a second date.

6.   Tell the kids to *grab* a snack before they leave for the football game.

7.   We can *catch* Mr. Smithers when we return from our Phoenix trip.

8.   Our boss is a *little rough around the edges* and has been known to make his staff members cry.

9.   You can *hang* in the bookstore *til* I finish the grocery shopping.

10.   I don't think our new contractor is *on the up and up*.

4, Bias in Writing   **Refer to the Handbook, pp. 132–133.**

Rewrite each of the following sentences to eliminate sexist terminology.

Example: Kathy Summers is a local fireman.

Answer: **Kathy Summers is a local firefighter.**

1. A police officer should always remember to wear his badge.

2. I will tip twenty percent to a waitress if she provides excellent service.

3. All the congressmen voted in favor of the bill.

4. The mailmen who work in California should wear a strong sunscreen every day.

5. Of all creatures on the planet, man is the most intelligent and the most destructive.

6. I hope the stewardess offers me more than peanuts on my next trip.

7. Any person who leaves early should leave his raffle ticket in the basket.

8. The job was so big that Laura was not sure our department had enough manpower to complete the work on time.

9. We are studying the work of black American authors in our English class.

10. Brian's mother is divorced and works full time as a dental assistant.

5, The Dictionary   **Refer to the Handbook, pp. 134–137.**

Use a dictionary to answer the following questions.

1. How many syllables are in *astronaut* and *emotional?* Write out both words and mark the syllable breaks.

2. Define *magazine* and explain the origin of the word.

3. What is the etymology of the word *manner?* What type of manner best exemplifies this origin?

4. What is the origin of the word *poet?*

5. How many syllables are in *porcupine?* Write out the word and mark the syllable breaks.

6. Check the etymology of the word *bait.* You will find that it is a particular form of a related word that is also found in English. What is that other word?

7. What are the two meanings of the noun *syllabuses?* What are the variant spellings of this word?

8. What is the origin of the name of the game *blackjack?*

9. How has the word *apron* changed over time? (Hint: What is faulty separation?) Give a similar word that did not undergo this same change.

10. What is it that makes a *March hare* mad?

6, The Thesaurus   **Refer to the Handbook, pp. 137–138.**

For each word given, use a thesaurus to find five or more synonyms and at least one antonym.
Indicate the part of speech for your entries.

Example: direct

Answer: Adjective: lying in a straight line; spoken freely

Verb: to control the course; to have charge of; to give   orders

antonym: (adjective) indirect

1. document

2. translate

3. end

4. foul

5. limit

6. riot

7. hot

8. maneuver

9. said

10. minister

SENTENCE PARTS AND PATTERNS

SENTENCES

1a, Verbs Refer to the Handbook, pp. 139–141.

For each of the sentences, underline the verb once. Then indicate if the verb expresses action or a state of being as follows:

- If the verb is linking, underline both the verb and the predicate adjective(s) or predicate noun(s) (VL, PA, PN).

- If the action verb is transitive, underline both the verb and the indirect or direct object(s) (VT, IO, DO).

- If the action verb is intransitive, underline only the verb (VI).

For example: Ollie cut the boards.
                 VT   DO

1. We climbed the mountain and reached the summit before sundown.

2. My sister Jane gave our parents a surprise fiftieth anniversary party.

3. The weather seems fine today.

4. We picked up a sandwich for lunch at the diner on the corner.

5. The sandwiches were delicious.

6. The server gave us a dessert menu.

7. My brother has invested most of his money in the stock market.

8. The professor wrote a book on his experience teaching college students.

9. My neighbor Dave is an agent for the Internal Revenue Service.

10. Family pets are prohibited in the hotel.

SENTENCES

1a, Nouns   **Refer to the Handbook, pp. 141–142.**

Complete the following table. Consult a dictionary if necessary.

For example:

	SINGULAR	PLURAL	SINGULAR POSSESSIVE	PLURAL POSSESSIVE
	Pen	**pens**	**pen's**	**pens'**
1.	lamp			
2.	apple			
3.	suitcase			
4.	doctor			
5.	shark			
6.	man			
7.	convertible			
8.	crowd			
9.	sky			
10.	society			

SENTENCES

1a, Pronouns   **Refer to the Handbook, pp. 142–143.**

Underline the pronouns in the following sentences.

For example: <u>I</u> wanted to invite Paul to the spaghetti dinner, but <u>he</u> is allergic to tomatoes.

1. Can you tell where I had the plastic surgery?

2. I fell asleep while Mr. White was giving his speech.

3. Carla usually has her hair styled before a big date.

4. The child had chocolate ice cream melting down his chin.

5. Can you tell me how to get to the apple orchard?

6. Give one piece of candy to each of your students.

7. Because I had a terrible cold, I did not visit my grandmother in the hospital.

8. Our teacher reminded us to begin our research papers early.

9. The judge thought her blackberry jam was better than mine.

10. These are the times that try men's souls.

SENTENCES

Choose the correct adjectival form (positive, comparative, or superlative) and underline your selection in each sentence that follows.

For example: Of all six children, Karen is the (old, older, <u>oldest</u>) one.

1. The Millennium Force is Cedar Point's (tall, taller, tallest) roller coaster.

2. The waves at Tanner Beach are (big, bigger, biggest) than those at West Beach and East Beach.

3. July 22, 1922 was the (hot, hotter, hottest) day ever recorded in Detroit, Michigan.

4. I cannot decide which is (delicious, more delicious, the most delicious)—the cannoli or the chocolate cream pie.

5. Before starting the race, the judge called, "May the (good, better, best) cyclist win!"

6. I have visited many state parks, and I still think Hartwick Pines State Park is (good, better, best).

7. The judges sampled all ten fudge recipes and decided that the vanilla pecan fudge was (creamy, creamier, creamiest).

8. Out of the four applicants, who is (good, better, best)?

9. We need to agree on who is the (great, greater, greatest) president—Abraham Lincoln, George Washington, or John Kennedy.

10. The kids thought Six Flags Amusement Park was (fun, more fun, the most fun) than the art museum.

SENTENCES

Underline the adverbs in the following sentences.

For example: He completed the test <u>more slowly</u> than the other fourth graders.

1. The finely chopped onions sizzled slowly in the frying pan.

2. Please sit quietly.

3. We were very happy to learn that Grandmother would arrive very shortly.

4. After the thunderstorm, steam rose eerily from the still-warm pavement.

5. The builders worked carefully and diligently to finish the biggest project of the year.

6. For a work so famous, Lincoln's "Gettysburg Address" is surprisingly short.

7. The solider climbed stealthily over the very rugged wall.

8. There is something fundamentally wrong with his theory.

9. The judge angrily scolded the very young lawyer for arriving late to court.

10. The vase of freshly cut peonies gave the room a wonderful smell.

SENTENCES

1a, Prepositions   **Refer to the Handbook, pp. 144.**

In the following sentences, enclose the complete prepositional phrases in parentheses and underline the prepositions.

For example: I walked (<u>to</u> the grocery, the fruit stand, and the bank).

1. Please leave the sauce simmering on the stove for thirty minutes.

2. Most dolphins have acute eyesight in the water.

3. All the Muscat grapes in the orchard were destroyed by frost.

4. We rode our bikes down the steep hill and into the next town.

5. Forty-seven stories above the street, the birds built their nest on one of the Chrysler Building's ledges.

6. After delivering the newspapers, Susan realized her hands were black with ink.

7. The snowstorm that came in from the East lasted for two days.

8. In the basket on the refrigerator, there are fresh towels and washcloths.

9. Chocolate amaretto is still one of my favorite flavors.

10. He pulled the crisp white shirt over his head and tucked it into his black trousers.

SENTENCES

In the following sentences, enclose the conjunction-containing clauses in parentheses. Then underline the conjunctions and label them as coordinating (COORD), subordinating (SUB), or correlative (CORREL).

For example: (<u>If</u> I had more money), I would replace my old car. (SUB)

1.   We paid for the popcorn and we went back to our seats.

2.   The earthquake shook the small village, but none of the villagers were injured.

3.   Although the lawyer was a Harvard Law School graduate, his fees were quite reasonable.

4.   Neither Kevin nor Sam wants to travel to the coast this weekend.

5.   Unless you sign the release form, your child will not be able to attend summer camp.

6.   I am excited to move to New York City, yet I fear I will miss the smell of the county.

7.   Outside the office it was hot and windy, but inside it was cool and quiet.

8.   My grandfather used to say, "You're either part of the solution or part of the problem."

9.   When we learned the concert tickets would cost four hundred dollars each, we cancelled our plans.

10.   Whether you enjoy steak or seafood, the Original Steakhouse is a great place to have dinner.

For each sentence that follows, underline the complete subject in the main clause.

For example: <u>The fact that my former boss and co-workers would also be at the wedding</u> was the reason we stayed home.

1. Billy's sense of humor kept the crowd laughing all night.

2. The neighbor's black and white pit bull, named Sly, always greets us with a wagging tail.

3. Mrs. Smith's fruit pies are on sale this week.

4. When the Canadian skiers reached the top of the mountain, they plotted their course down.

5. The last time I checked, the university had five libraries.

6. Resting by the side of the road, some bicyclists from the tour were eating their lunches.

7. Branagh's remakes of *Henry V* and *Much Ado About Nothing* have brought Shakespeare to new audiences.

8. The orange and red tulips from Denmark towered over our domestic tulips.

9. Due to record rainfall, the Mississippi River and its many tributaries rose to record levels in 1993.

10. The new anti-smoking law in Michigan will go into effect sometime in May of 2010.

SENTENCES

Underline the complete predicate in the main clause of each of the following sentences.

For example: I <u>felt the idea for a surprise party was not a good idea.</u>

1. Smoking is expensive and addictive.

2. Jerry wanted to attend medical school on the East Coast.

3. The manager was skilled at calming angry customers.

4. The soldiers received their orders and prepared for life in Afghanistan.

5. After working together all day, Bill and Ted cooked dinner together also.

6. The State Fair earns revenue for both the county and the state.

7. Although I have to write two book reports, I still want to go shopping with you.

8. Raoulito was happy he had backed up his hard disk when it crashed only a day later.

9. The pizza deliveryman was shocked that we gave him such a large tip.

10. Though Eliza lived on the sixth floor, she created a garden of tomatoes, lettuce, onions, and herbs by planting seeds in window boxes.

SENTENCES

1b, Objects   **Refer to the Handbook, pp. 147.**

In the following sentences, underline the object(s), and then indicate whether it is a direct object (DO) or an indirect object (IO).

For example: My children bought <u>me</u> <u>a mother's ring</u> for my birthday.

IO   DO

1. Tamara threw the flowers in Jack's face.

2. My boss loves money.

3. The bank robbers terrorized the customers and stole the money.

4. The mother hid the chips and cookies in the back cupboard.

5. Julia asked me to take her to the mall.

6. The teacher gave the students five pencils and two notebooks at the beginning of the school year.

7. The children offered the teacher candy at the class party.

8. The babysitter gave the boy a stuffed teddy bear and then told him a story.

9. Jerry mastered karate.

10. He planned a surprise party for her.

SENTENCES

1c, Prepositional Phrases.   **Refer to the Handbook, pp. 148.**

In the following sentences, place parentheses ( ) around the prepositional phrase(s).

For example: We all preferred the cake with the butter cream frosting.

We all preferred the cake (with the butter cream frosting).

1. The girl hid under the bed until her mother came home.

2. To get to the grocery store, go over the next hill to the end of the street and turn left.

3. The hot sauce on the table will make you cry.

4. The car with the dent on the front fender is my sister's.

5. The temperature in the hockey stadium is dropping fast.

6. The daffodils are just blooming in early spring.

7. I saw gleam in his eyes when his wife walked in the door.

8. I never guessed that the cat would be hiding in the closet in the hallway.

9. In the future, I would like you to ask permission before you borrow my car.

10. The dog ran to his dish, ate his food quickly, and ran to get his toys.

1c, Verbals   **Refer to the Handbook, pp. 148–149.**

In the following sentences, underline the verbals and verbal phrases. Then identify their type as gerund (GER), infinitive (INF), past participle (PAST PART), or present participle (PRES PART).

For example: <u>Considering how little money we raised</u>, I think we should only serve desserts at the next meeting. (PRES PART)

1. The girl selling cookies door-to-door plans to stay on her side of town.

2. Pacing yourself during an exam is crucial.

3. The man plowing the street is not wearing a hat or gloves.

4. The Continental Army, faced with many hardships, managed to defeat the better trained and equipped British.

5. To request more funding, you will need to speak with the president of the company.

6. Making the perfect chocolate chip cookie requires real butter dark brown sugar.

7. I noticed the drawing on the back of the building.

8. My grandmother always urged me to believe in myself.

9. Feeling the wind come up suddenly, Maggie suspected that a thunderstorm was approaching.

10. His favorite hobbies are snorkeling and fishing.

1d, Clauses   **Refer to the Handbook, pp. 149–151.**

Underline and label the adjective (relative) clauses (ADJ CLS), adverb clauses (ADV CLS), and noun clauses (NOUN CLS) in the following sentences.

For example: The fish <u>that live in our lake</u> have been reduced in number recently by an increase in the cormorant population. (**ADJ CLS**)

1. The tennis player, who injured his knee during the last match, is forfeiting.

2. I realized that Joe was an ungrateful boyfriend who would be eating alone tonight.

3. The antique was damaged after we moved.

4. Before I leave for France, I want to contact the post office to stop my mail.

5. After losing three games straight, the team was ecstatic when it beat the undefeated first place team.

6. I felt uneasy when I learned one of our staff members, who had been stealing money from the company, was fired.

7. My motorcycle was magnificent when it ran but a great frustration the rest of the time.

8. Whoever read the novel, which is over seven hundred pages long, should be proud.

9. He knew a good deal when he saw it.

10. The pond at the State Park, where the Canadian geese flock, is now contaminated and closed off to the public.

SENTENCES

1e, Types of Sentences   **Refer to the Handbook, pp. 151–152.**

Classify each of the following sentences by type: simple, compound, complex, or compound-complex.

For example: I rolled out the dough, and my mom stuffed it with ricotta cheese. (**compound**)

1. Though I exercise every day, I still cannot lose those final ten pounds.

2. Bill runs in Central Park.

3. Joe will travel to Africa this summer, and his children will stay with their grandparents in Rhode Island.

4. After scooping ice cream all summer, my right arm was so strong that I could beat my older brother in arm wrestling, and my left arm looked so withered to me that it seemed almost like the forelegs of *Tyrannosaurus rex*.

5. The alligator stared at us from the swampy waters, but we felt safe on the boat.

6. Frogs are vulnerable amphibians and have many natural defenses.

7. Antonia went from meeting to meeting until three o'clock, and then she caught a cab to the airport for her four o'clock flight.

8. Becky saw her photograph posted on the Internet, and she felt her privacy had been violated.

9. Kelly saw that her ex-boyfriend had posted an unflattering picture of her on Facebook, so she called him and threatened to do the same.

10. The weather in Italy this time of year can be brutally hot.

2, Subject-Verb Agreement 1   **Refer to the Handbook, pp. 152–157.**

Correct the errors in subject-verb agreement in the following sentences.

For example: The cost of all the new doors were more than we expected.

Correction: **The cost of all the new doors was more than we expected.**

1. The ticket, including dinner with dessert, a floor show, and dancing after, cost only twenty dollars.

2. There is usually some teachers who are willing to chaperone the prom.

3. Neither the potato salad nor the fruit salad were very cold.

4. The Civil War exhibit and The Revolutionary War documentary offers a glimpse into the past.

5. High tides and wind creates dangerous conditions along the coast.

6. Fourteen aunts, uncles, and cousins, except for Gramma Gump, was coming to our cookout.

7. The spaghetti dinner fundraiser bring in four thousand dollars every year.

8. All the houses on King Street is too expensive for the young couple.

9. The fourth graders at Elmwood Elementary School has been practicing The Pledge of Allegiance.

10. Congress need to vote on the Health Care Bill by March 18, 2010.

2e–l, Subject-Verb Agreement 2   **Refer to the Handbook, pp. 155–157.**

Correct the errors in subject-verb agreement in the following sentences.

For example: All of the athletes who earned medals stands on the field for a picture.

Correction: All of the athletes who earned medals stand on the field for a picture.

1.   Anything you donate go to a good cause.

2.   Dave is the only one at the party who always leave early.

3.   None of my classes meet before 10 a.m.

4.   There is, though our firm tries to hide it, financial difficulties.

5.   Politics both fascinate and repulse him.

6.   Credit cards that charges over twenty-one percent interest should be put through the shredder.

7.   *Profiles in Courage* were written by John F. Kennedy.

8.   One of favorite desserts are Bananas Foster.

9.   Whether John will pass the Michigan Bar Exam this time are unknown.

10.   Last year, one of my cousins were on American Idol.

SENTENCES

3a–b, Principal Parts of Irregular Verbs   **Refer to the Handbook, pp. 157–159.**

Correct the misuse of irregular verbs in the following sentences.

For example: When the wind picked up, it blowed out the candle.

Correction: **When the wind picked up, it blew out the candle.**

1.   If you bent the pipe more, I think it will fit.

2.   The squirrels digged in the garden looking for radishes.

3.   The senator speaked last week at the Democratic fundraiser.

4.   The patient had been striked with the swine flu before his surgery.

5.   I seen that new movie with Robert Pattinson last week.

6.   I had wrote to him all summer, but he only replied with a single postcard.

7.   When the bell rung, the lecturer began immediately.

8.   The prisoners were hung at sundown.

9.   Many flowers and wreaths are lain at the Vietnam Memorial every day.

10.   After he had stole the video game, he was overcome with feelings of guilt.

SENTENCES

Rewrite the sentence provided in the verb tenses indicated.

For example: The chef worked at Perry's Chop House in Detroit for two years.

Present Perfect: The chef has worked at Perry's Chop House in Detroit for two years.

The sun rises over the horizon every morning.

1.   Present Perfect:

2.   Present Progressive:

3.   Present Perfect Progressive:

4.   Past:

5.   Past Perfect:

6.   Past Progressive:

7.   Past Perfect Progressive:

8.   Future:

9.   Future Perfect:

10.   Future Progressive:

11.   Future Perfect Progressive:

SENTENCES

Write, in the parentheses provided, the mood of the underlined clause.

For example:

(   )   <u>If I could travel anywhere I wanted,</u> I would travel to Rome.

(subjunctive)   <u>If I could travel anywhere I wanted,</u> I would travel to Rome.

1. (   )   Bob asked <u>that Joe come early today</u>.

2. (   )   <u>Clean your room and take out the trash.</u>

3. (   )   <u>Every night he reads until bedtime.</u>

4. (   )   Mary said, "<u>Hurry up, or we'll miss the bus.</u>"

5. (   )   <u>I wished I would win the lottery,</u> but I was unlucky.

6. (   )   Lili said <u>her voice was similar to Sheryl Crow's.</u>

7. (   )   <u>If I were ten years younger,</u> I would attempt the triathlon.

8. (   )   <u>Can you tell me the time?</u>

9. (   )   <u>If it were up to me,</u> I'd change the policy.

10. (   )   "<u>Knock on the door three times before you enter,</u>" she said.

SENTENCES

3f, Active and Passive Voices   **Refer to the Handbook, pp. 164–165.**

Rewrite each sentence, changing its voice (that is, rewrite sentences in the passive voice to the active voice, and vice versa). Indicate the voice used in your rewritten sentence.

Example: *American Idol is* watched by people of all ages.

Rewritten: (active) People of all ages watch *American Idol.*

1.   A report was written by the executive committee.

2.   The students in Ms. Biddle's class played chess.

3.   The teenager girls in the bookstore loved the book titled *Twilight.*

4.   Regina saw the Blue Line bus.

5.   The World Series is watched by many people who rarely watch baseball otherwise.

6.   The party snacks and desserts were enjoyed by all the conference attendees.

7.   The renovation plans were developed by the Harding-Mott Construction Company.

8.   Our guide called the tallest redwood the "Mother of the Forest."

9.   A quilting demonstration was given by the head seamstress at Mervin's Fabric Store.

10.   The firefighters hoisted the ladder to the top of the burning building.

4a, Pronoun Agreement   Refer to the Handbook, pp. 165–167.

Correct the errors in pronoun-antecedent agreement in the following sentences.

For example: If any student needs an extra ticket to the dance, please tell them to call the office.

The problem: *any student* is singular, *them* is plural. There are many possible solutions; here are two:

> If any student needs an extra ticket to the dance, please tell him or her to call the office.
>
> (grammatically correct but somewhat awkward)
>
> If students need extra tickets to the dance, please tell them to call the office.
>
> (switch to the plural *students*, which allows the use of the plural pronoun *them*.)

1. The jury provided their decision to the judge.

2. Every morning Buster frightens the mail carrier, Joe, which is afraid of dogs.

3. Neither the cook nor the server pay for his own meal.

4. When Louisa and Hal come to visit, they always bring his and her dog.

5. Each man worked on their soccer skills.

6. The orchestra will open their twenty-eighth season with tonight's performance.

7. The band will go on strike if they do not get a raise.

8. My brother's hamster, who is calico colored, is named Rascal.

9. A doctor needs to be calm when talking to their patients.

10. If anyone wants to come to the banquet, they will need to pay before Friday.

SENTENCES

4b, Pronoun Reference   **Refer to the Handbook, pp. 167–168.**

Correct the vague or confusing pronoun references in the following sentences.

For example: Kelly told her boss that she needed to submit the budget report today.

The problem: Who needs to submit the budget report, Kelly or her boss? There are many possible solutions; here is one:

Kelly said, "Ms.Jones, can you submit the budget report today?"

1. That could be a problem.

2. My husband, who grows a beautiful vegetables, eats it every day.

3. Though I know that supply-side economics focuses on production, and demand-side economics emphasizes consumption, this has never helped me understand where my paycheck goes every week.

4. If my medical insurance company denies the claim, they will be speaking to my attorney.

5. When tours come through our town, they often stop at the Shelburne Museum, where you can see an extensive American folk art collection.

6. The diner serves the best western omelet, so they rarely eat breakfast at home.

7. On the radio, it said that the hurricane will touch land early tomorrow morning.

8. Cormac McCarthy's *All the Pretty Horses* combines ample description with sparse dialog, and it creates a sense of the lone horseman riding through the vast, southwestern landscape.

9. Because Brian and Ned try to eat healthy every day, certain people do not need to diet.

10. Last summer I went to college in England, which required weekly exams.

SENTENCES

4c, Pronoun Case 1   Refer to the Handbook, pp. 169–172.

Correct the pronoun case errors in the following sentences.

For example: The woman on the right is her.

Correction: **The woman on the right is she.**

1.   Have you seen mine brother?

2.   My sister and me went to the new shopping center.

3.   According to Julia and I, Pizza Pit has the best pizza in town.

4.   The boss appreciated them working on Saturday night.

5.   My sister said she would be going to visit our grandmother after visiting Susan and I.

6.   The boy who stole the puppy is him.

7.   Us getting such high scores on the ACT is why our class had a pizza party.

8.   Her and me studied for the exam with Tom, Rico, and Zino.

9.   The doctor asked she and her mother to wait outside.

10.   Because the book was written by she and I, we split the royalty check in half.

SENTENCES

Correct the pronoun case errors in the following sentences.

For example: My cousin enjoys Pilates class more than me.

Correction: My cousin enjoys Pilates class more than I.

1. The attorney asked my mother and I to sit down before he read the will.

2. Despite all his campaigning, the incumbent was running stronger than him, as the *New York Times* reported.

3. The teacher called Denny, Mindy and I to the front of the classroom.

4. My sister, whom has incredibly acute hearing when it comes to the telephone, yelled out from the shower, "Who is that call for?"

5. Free pine tree saplings will be given to whomever asks.

6. The judge and her will have a private meeting in the judge's chamber.

7. My brother and I are avid readers, but he hasn't read as many books as me this summer.

8. The winners of the poetry contest, my brother and me, received a gift certificate to Barnes and Noble.

9. I forget her name, but the Oscar for Best Actress went to whomever played the mother in *The Blind Side.*

10. *Twilight* was written by who?

5, Adjectives and Adverbs   **Refer to the Handbook, pp. 173-176.**

Correct the errors in adjective and adverb usage in the following sentences.

For example: The sales clerk looked angrily.

Correction: The sales clerk looked angry.

1. The caterer felt badly that the food was cold and undercooked.

2. That green blouse looks well with your new black jacket.

3. Stretch your legs good before you start the race.

4. The professor looked curious at their group project.

5. With two of their starters on the disabled list, things look badly for the Seattle Mariners.

6. The steadily increase in sales before the holidays was offset by their declining steadily for the six months after the holidays.

7. After receiving a below average performance rating from her boss, Julie was feeling badly.

8. You will need to finish the project quick because the client will be here on Friday.

9. The chocolate cream pie tastes incredibly.

10. Even though Elaine was a healthy thirty-four-year-old who had always eaten good, each Thanksgiving her grandmother said she looked a little thin.

SENTENCES

6, Sentence Fragments 1   Refer to the Handbook, pp. 176–179.

For each of the following entries, indicate whether it is a fragment (F) or a complete sentence (S). Your answer may refer to part of the entry or the entire entry. If the entry is a fragment, change it so it is a complete sentence.

Example: After I planted two flats of purple petunias.

Answer: F; After I planted two flats of purple petunias, a frost warning was issued.

1. Despite the hours of work he committed to the project

2. I went home.

3. As long as you support your point.

4. A local dance troop will perform at the banquet tonight.

5. The cat that climbed the tree. It is a stray.

6. To train ten weeks for the triathlon and then break an ankle.

7. Thousands of ants spilled out of the hole.

8. You have to do the laundry. Before you go to work.

9. Watching the events of the car accident ahead. Maxine almost had an accident herself.

10. It came to our attention. That Mike was certified in first aid.

6, Sentence Fragments 2   **Refer to the Handbook, pp. 176–179.**

Rewrite the following sentences to eliminate sentence fragments.

For example: The children love stories before bed. Also cookies and milk.

Correction: The children love stories and cookies and milk before bed.

  1. The boy loves his great aunt. And visits every day.

  2. My big brother Todd likes to dance. Especially to hip-hop music.

  3. The menu highlighted my two favorite meals. Shrimp scampi and seafood Alfredo.

  4. My husband and I bought tickets for the Billy Joel concert; My brother and his wife, too.

  5. When I saw the *Mona Lisa* in person. I was, to be honest, disappointed.

  6. The company's health care costs have increased by twenty-five percent. Which is a huge drain on the budget.

  7. Writing a good essay is time consuming. But is necessary to pass the class.

  8. The library wants to sponsor a poetry contest. For the fourth-, fifth- and sixth-grade students.

  9. Gertrude is my closest friend. Even though she moved to Poland.

10. I teach classes during the fall and winter semesters. But not summer.

SENTENCES

7, Comma Splices 1   **Refer to the Handbook, pp. 179–182.**

Rewrite the following sentences to eliminate comma splices, using a different method to correct each sentence.

For example: I ate six slices of pizza, I was hungry.

Correction: I ate six slices of pizza because I was hungry.

Correction: Because I was hungry, I ate six slices of pizza.

Correction: I ate six slices of pizza; I was hungry.

Correction: I ate six slices of pizza. I was hungry.

 1. The price of plane tickets is rising, I hope I saved enough money.

 2. Professor Gerson has a pleasantly acid sense of humor, he quipped that the term *European ally* is an oxymoron.

 3. The music is too loud turn it down.

 4. The man was arrested as he arrived home he was charged with armed robbery.

 5. The backpackers were prepared for any type of weather, they were glad to have brought their rain gear.

 6. Picasso's work has been classified into periods, perhaps best known is his Blue Period.

 7. We were out of eggs, we baked the cake anyway.

 8. My roommate reported that my old sneakers had begun to move on their own, he said they were a violation of U.S. treaties banning the development of biological weapons.

 9. I want you to meet my husband we have been married for twenty years.

10. The server spilled the wine and dropped the rolls I think he needs a new job.

7, Comma Splices 2   **Refer to the Handbook, pp. 179–182.**

Rewrite the following sentences to eliminate comma splices, using a different method to correct each sentence.

For example: The morning was cold and rainy I stayed in bed.

Correction: Because the morning was cold and rainy, I stayed in bed.

Correction: The morning was cold and rainy, so I stayed in bed.

Correction: The morning was cold and rainy. I stayed in bed.

Correction: The morning was cold and rainy; I stayed in bed.

1. We studied about the witch hunt in Europe the class had many misconceptions about witches.

2. With all the channel choices on cable and satellite TV these days, I wish there was something good to watch, it seems like there were better programs when I had fewer choices.

3. Only take one dessert, we have a large crowd tonight.

4. They weren't important ideas, they were interesting suggestions.

5. I'm not sure if we should purchase the house now I think housing prices will fall next month.

6. Charles Dickens is my favorite author, *A Tale of Two Cities* is my favorite book.

7. When I play video games, I like to pretend I am involved in the action, it helps me imagine the next move.

8. The boy is too young to go swimming alone, his parents will need to supervise.

9. The children can watch videos in the basement, the parents can play cards in the kitchen, the teenagers can eat pizza on the back porch.

10. The accountant has made a serious error, he will not have a job tomorrow.

SENTENCES

Rewrite the following to eliminate fused or run-on sentences.

For example: I went back for a second helping of mom's lasagna it was delicious.

Correction: I went back for a second helping of mom's lasagna; it was delicious.

1. The large trout jerked on the hook fiercely it broke the line and swam away.

2. I like spaghetti and meatballs I rarely eat in Italian restaurants.

3. I have been indoors all week I feel like lying in the sun.

4. I know what an armadillo looks like I'm not quite sure what an aardvark looks like.

5. The last U.S. space shuttle flight to *Mir* was made in 1999, since then all shuttle flights have been to the new International Space Station.

6. Pet owners need to clean up after their pets there is five hundred dollar fine.

7. The party starts in five minutes we need to leave right now.

8. When I visited Maria over the holidays, I met many of her high school friends they were very friendly.

9. Be honest do you think my chocolate cake is better than grandma's chocolate cake?

10. We hiked the last hour in the pouring rain our equipment is completely soaked with water.

SENTENCES

Rewrite the following to eliminate fused or run-on sentences.

For example: I felt at ease when I met the president he shook my hand and winked at me.

Correction: I felt as ease when I met the president because he shook my hand and winked at me.

1. We packed peanut butter and jelly sandwiches we also brought apples.

2. The veal parmesan was excellent the dessert was excellent as well.

3. Janel got an A on her essay she must have written many drafts.

4. The preschoolers boarded the bus after the zoo tour the parents fell asleep on the way home.

5. During the snowstorm, the city workers plowed the streets the citizens shoveled the sidewalks.

6. My parents retired then they moved to Florida.

7. The seamstress altered the bridal gown the bride held her breath.

8. Fish make great pets they require little care.

9. The beagle puppies are fun to watch they chase each other, barking in tiny voices.

10. The movie lasted for three hours most of the children fell asleep.

PUNCTUATION

1a–c, The Comma 1   **Refer to the Handbook, pp. 183–186.**

In the following sentences, correct the comma errors by adding or removing commas.

For example: I packed my bags with only the essentials and I called a taxi for a ride to the airport.

Correction: I packed my bags with only the essentials, and I called a taxi for a ride to the airport.

1. As I felt the warm water hit my skin I closed my eyes and took a deep breath.

2. I have known Bob all my life yet I am not sure where he works.

3. Laughing the teenagers piled into a small booth.

4. The best dessert on the menu the tiramisu is sold out tonight.

5. My oldest brother Geoffrey usually comes for Thanksgiving.

6. Running over the garden hose for the second time my neighbor thought about installing a sprinkler system.

7. Because we want to attract more customers we raffle a prize every week.

8. Driving in the Indianapolis 500 which is one of America's premier races, was an immense thrill for Sharleen.

9. Considering both the price of gasoline and the price of a hotel we decided to skip our annual vacation.

10. Having gotten lost twice already Doug thought it would be wise to ask for directions at the service station.

1d–g, The Comma 2   **Refer to the Handbook, pp. 186–188.**

In the following sentences, correct the comma errors by adding or removing commas.

For example: Go to the fruit stand and buy peaches strawberries, and cantaloupe.

Correction: Go to the fruit stand and buy peaches, strawberries, and cantaloupe.

1. The car was described as having, tinted windows a sunroof, and a red pinstripe.

2. This fall Eliot was reading Ernest Hemingway, Maya Angelou and Alice Walker.

3. Because they did not honor the contract we will not do business with them again.

4. President Jimmy Carter may turn out to be more effective out of office than in unlike Lyndon Johnson.

5. Eating plenty of fiber will help you feel full lose weight and improve digestion.

6. John was elected by his peers to lead the team, and therefore feels both honored and pressured.

7. There are many healthy desserts for example that will fit into your diet plan.

8. As the workweek has been shortened, productivity has increased not decreased.

9. Our new chemistry teacher is smart funny and easy to understand.

10. Only a few students however wanted to take a field trip to the art museum.

PUNCTUATION

1h–l, The Comma 3   Refer to the Handbook, pp. 188–189.

Correct the errors by adding commas in the following sentences.

For example: Jenny called out "Run Forrest! Run!"

Correction: Jenny called out, "Run Forrest! Run!"

1. I smiled and said, "Yes, I'll be there."

2. If you want to call Jessica has a phone.

3. Our spring break runs from Monday March 15 through Monday March 22.

4. My sister called yesterday and asked "Guess who is having a baby?"

5. Lonnie gave me a ride from Tulsa Oklahoma to Paris Texas.

6. While I cook the pasta you sauté the mushrooms and onions.

7. Heidi comes in during the lunch rush and Brad comes in after the lunch rush.

8. "Your wife will love some red roses," said the vendor.

9. The senator's aides said their office had received more than 1400 letters in favor of the bill.

10. My new address is 4459 Summer Lane Sterling Heights MI 48066.

1m, The Comma 4   Refer to the Handbook, pp. 189–191.

Correct the following sentences by removing unnecessary commas.

For example: Perhaps, you could give yoga class another chance.

Correction: **Perhaps you could give yoga class another chance.**

1. The two water spaniels, and their owner, swam across the pond and dried off in the hot sun.

2. To my Aunt, Mary, my youngest brother could do no wrong.

3. Larry and Anna Marie did not like dogs, until, they met Buster.

4. You should, probably, use a strong sunscreen before you go to the beach.

5. The small, gold, locket was a family heirloom.

6. She poured the tea, into delicate tea cups, and served crumpets, and scones.

7. Kevin, played the lottery, but his wife played bingo.

8. Sell, sell, and sell, was the store's motto.

9. He, opened the roll, buttered it and savored the fresh aroma.

10. She loved to go to the museum, on Saturday, but he, preferred Sunday.

PUNCTUATION

2, The Semicolon   **Refer to the Handbook, pp. 191–192.**

Correct the following sentences by either adding or removing semicolons as appropriate. Some sentences may be correct as given.

For example: The children devoured the pizza, chips, and pop they had not eaten all day.

Correction: **The children devoured the pizza, chips, and pop; they had not eaten all day.**

1. I waited in line for four hours to get the tickets; but I didn't mind; nor did my sister.

2. The rapid decrease in computer hardware prices has put pressure on software developers to do the same, nonetheless, they have resisted the trend for the most part.

3. On one recent weekend I saw *Pearl Harbor*, which used extensive computer-generated simulations of an historical event, *The Matrix*, which explored virtual worlds accessed via mind control, and *Until the End of the World*, which presented computer-driven dream exploration.

4. I planted the sickly looking plant in the spring, it blossomed into a beautiful flowering shrub by summer.

5. Because there are so many errors when I use my GPS; I prefer and hand written map.

6. I married Andy when I was only eighteen; and because of this, I feel I missed some of my childhood.

7. My family took a raft trip down the Colorado River; which is rated 9 of a possible 10 in terms of difficulty.

8. I will try to settle the disagreement between Heather and Kim; but I don't think it will help.

9. The birthday cake I ordered for John Jr. was not only the wrong flavor but it was also dry I should have demanded my money back.

10. I loved the social aspect of high school such as the dances and football games, however, I would not want to go back there.

PUNCTUATION

3, The Colon   **Refer to the Handbook, pp. 193–194.**

Correct the following sentences by either adding or removing colons as appropriate. Some sentences may be correct as given. Remember that sometimes a colon can take the place of other punctuation.

For example: When the family moved out of the house next door, they left behind everything they did not want; four bicycles, an old trampoline, a broken lawn mower, and about ten outdoor cats.

Correction: **When the family moved out of the house next door, they left behind everything they did not want: four bicycles, an old trampoline, a broken lawn mower, and about ten outdoor cats.**

1. Remember our mission statement, "We help students develop the skills to become independent, self-sufficient adults who contribute to society."

2. Scientists, in an effort to isolate what it is in food that makes most people evaluate it as "tasting good or delicious," have determined the single most important ingredient, fat.

3. When you go to the grocery store please purchase: bread, butter, eggs and chocolate milk.

4. The conditions are perfect for planting flowers; rich soil, plenty of sunshine, and a forecast for rain.

5. We took the following route, Route 80 to Rock Springs, Route 187 to Farson, and Route 28 to South Pass City.

6. Joe has had three professions in his life, a used car salesman, a teacher and a lawyer.

7. There is one reason I never visit Key Largo. My ex husband lives there.

8. Professor Thomason argued that there was one reason the United States had not acted more decisively in Bosnia, it has no oil.

9. After the Morning Prayer, Pastor Steve asked the congregation to turn to Mark 1, 3.

10. The entrees on the menu include: vegetable lasagna, shrimp scampi, sirloin steak, and barbeque ribs.

4, The Apostrophe   **Refer to the Handbook, pp. 194-196.**

Correct the following sentences by either adding or removing apostrophes as appropriate.

For example: We went with the Smith Family. We are the Smiths good friends.

Correction: **We went with the Smith Family. We are the Smiths' good friends.**

1. We have forty dogs at the dog kennel, and we trim every dogs fur for the summer weather.

2. My grandmother told me that the '38 hurricane was much worse than this years storm.

3. We watched the bird make it's nest from the dryer lint.

4. The comedians humor fell flat with the late night crowd.

5. I thought it was her's, but perhaps its really Bills.

6. Dr. Barlows persuasive speech on the impact of diet on our health made me change my eating habits.

7. The soldiers weapon was lost in the battle.

8. Whose in charge of this event?

9. Their the only two employees who have a key to the safe.

10. I have trouble reading your writing because your bs' look like ps'.

| 5, Quotation Marks | Refer to the Handbook, pp. 197–199. |

Correct the following sentences by either adding, altering, or removing quotation marks and related punctuation as appropriate.

For example: Our teacher said S.E. Hinton's book *The Outsiders* was written when she was only sixteen years old.

Correction: **Our teacher said, "S.E. Hinton's book *The Outsiders* was written when she was only sixteen years old."**

1. "Where you place your commas is one of my teacher's "pet peeves", so I always double-check my work", said Elaine.

2. "Where would you like us to place the new furniture" asked the movers.

3. My favorite two poems are The Mending Wall by Robert Frost and A Shady Friend by Emily Dickinson.

4. Do not confuse the word implicit with the word explicit.

5. "Do you think the train ride to Chicago will be boring, asked Carl.

   "No, I replied. I will bring crossword puzzles, books and some snacks.

   What can I bring asked Carl?

6. Last year when I reread the book, "*To Kill a Mockingbird*", I discovered it was much more interesting than I ever remembered it to be.

7. The most difficult chapter of our history book, The American Constitution, is also the longest.

8. Lawrence had mixed feelings about hearing the president quoting from the Eagles' song Take It to the Limit. Was this the movie "The Big Chill" come to life?

9. The YMCA dedicated the new pool to its main benefactor, "Maybelle Kay Nelson."

10. "How many calories are in a medium hot fudge sundae,"? asked my mom.

PUNCTUATION

6a, The Period   **Refer to the Handbook, pp. 199–201.**

Correct the errors in the use of the period in the following sentences.

For example: Ms. Smith asked me if I could babysit the twins this Saturday?

Correction: Ms. Smith asked me if I could babysit the twins this Saturday.

1. Dr Craig is one of the most respected plastic surgeons in Michigan.

2. F.E.M.A. is an agency of the United States Department of Homeland Security.

3. I wondered if he knew what the U.S.D.A. stamp on the meat stood for.

4. When addressing a letter, the state of Florida is abbreviated as F.L.

5. Tintin's best friend is Capt Horatio Haddock.

6. The company changed its name from Cargo and Tate Investments to Cargo, Inc..

7. Do not bring electronic devices, such as iPods, cell phones, *etc,* to the testing area?

8. Please turn in your bible to John 11/ch. 3 to 4.

9. The graduation ceremony will be on Friday, Jan 9.

10. Jerry asked me what time I had arrived at work this morning?

6b–c. The Question Mark and Exclamation Point   Refer to the Handbook, pp. 201–202.

Correct the errors in the use of the question mark and exclamation point in the following sentences.

For example: When will the Easter eggs be done boiling.

Correction: **When will the Easter eggs be done boiling?**

1. The bus driver asked, "Is there anyone on the bus who lives at the end of Cole Street."

2. John exclaimed, "I have the winning ticket."

3. Which route to Des Moines has less traffic, John wanted to know?

4. "Why do you always throw your coffee grounds in the garden."

5. My boss asked me whether I wanted to be on the blue team or the green team?

6. Rolf asked me, "What is the difference between a CD and CD-ROM."

7. "Ouch," he screamed. "Get off my foot."

8. Whose red sandals were left on the boat.

9. "Do you mind printing another report," asked Mr. Jenkins.

10. I could not remember when they were coming?

PUNCTUATION

6d–h, Other Punctuation   **Refer to the Handbook, pp. 202–206.**

Correct the punctuation errors involving the use of the dash, period, question mark, exclamation point, parentheses, brackets, ellipses, and the slash in the following sentences.

For example: Bugs Bunny and The Road Runner; the two most famous cartoon adversaries from the 1960s; have been popular with three generations.

Correction: Bugs Bunny and The Road Runner—the two most famous cartoon adversaries from the 1960s—have been popular with three generations.
OR
Bugs Bunny and The Road Runner, also known as the two most famous cartoon adversaries from the 1960s, have been popular with three generations.

1. Barack Obama the current president of The United States is our forty-fourth president.

2. When in Rome (as the saying goes) do as the Romans do.

3. Maya Angelou's beautiful words hit home: "A bird doesn't sing because it has an answer…. it sings because it has a song."

4. "Our class meets in that new science building. What's its name? Something Hall … . Burstein … . Gurstein? I can't remember," said John.

5. I still remember the opening lines of Shakespeare's Sonnet LXXIII:

    "That time of year thou mayst in me behold When yellow leaves, or none, or few, do hang

    Upon those boughs which shake against the cold."

6. This is a beautiful house to raise a family if you're a millionaire.

7. Ask the librarian; an expert in records of the past; if he knows the history of the old bank building.

83

8. I loved eating at the late night buffet on the cruise ship, until I got home and stepped on the scale.

9. The lecture, a ninety-minute torrent of anecdotes, facts, figures, and numerous slides, left me exhilarated but exhausted.

10. All the work I did to prepare the garden, pull the weeks, till the soil, erect the fence, made me wake up the next day with a sore back and calloused hands.

VIII MECHANICS

MECHANICS

| 1a–d, Capitals 1 | Refer to the Handbook, pp. 207–210. |

Correct the errors in capitalization in the following sentences.

For example: We visited the smithsonian institution during our trip to washington, dc.

Correction: **We visited the Smithsonian Institution during our trip to Washington, DC.**

1. People who live in the South are more comfortable with hot weather.

2. When James "joe" Jackson sang last week at the hartford ave grill, the crowd roared its approval.

3. The sky was so clear last night that we could see the north star.

4. The women's conference will feature several famous african American authors.

5. In the last four months, the missouri and mississippi rivers reached record flood levels, but the hudson river was below normal.

6. I only use jell-o brand gelatin when I make my desserts.

7. We offered to take the items not sold at the auction to the salvation army on cole street.

8. The republican party should gain two more seats in the senate in the upcoming election.

9. Once labor day weekend rolls around, you know that Summer is really over.

10. Julie is catholic, but her husband is jewish.

1e–j, Capitals 2   **Refer to the Handbook, pp. 210–212.**

Correct the errors in capitalization in the following sentences.

For example: When I received an outstanding evaluation, I was happy. no, I was ecstatic.

Correction: **When I received an outstanding evaluation, I was happy. No, I was ecstatic.**

1. In a recent article, commentator Julia Webb wrote, "for the first time in U.S. history, by the year 2002, more than 50 percent of all American jobs will require at least one year of college."

2. Did you read Mitch Albom's article in today's *detroit news*?

3. My favorite courses this term are english, Calculus and History.

4. I think she bought one of the new Apple Notebook Computers.

5. The News Media program I watch the most is the *o'reilly factor* on fox news channel.

6. Have you read a *tale of two cities* by charles dickens?

7. Our city has two Mosques, four Temples, and twenty-eight Churches, twelve of which are catholic.

8. Our family is planning a trip to england, where we will tour the tower of london and the british museum.

9. The tuition rates at Public Universities are rising every year. The university of minnesota will raise tuition by 7.5 percent next year.

10. Six children in the fourth grade have been diagnosed with adhd.

MECHANICS

2, Abbreviations   **Refer to the Handbook, pp. 212–214.**

Correct the errors in the use of abbreviations in the following sentences.

For example: Between 2008 and 2009, housing prices dropped by 15 pct.

Correction: Between 2008 and 2009, housing prices dropped by 15 percent.

1.   Our history teacher asked us to read ch. 18 before class tomorrow.

2.   The new dept. chair will be here next week. She is from N.Y. City.

3.   Aristotle was born in B.C. 384.

4.   According to the town historian, the house was built c. 1900.

5.   You will need to order four doz. company shirts for the team conference.

6.   The dissolution of the Soviet Union has generated much debate over the future of N.A.T.O.

7.   If we leave now, we'll get home in the p.m.

8.   The only classes I need to finish my degree are psych and soc.

9.   The bus leaves at 9 am from Sixth Ave.

10.   British & American English differ in many small ways; e.g., we place a period after the abbreviation for *Mister* (Mr.), whereas the British do not.

3, Numbers   Refer to the Handbook, pp. 214–216.

Correct the errors in the use of numbers in the following sentences.

For example: There are 26 new flavors at the ice cream shop.

Correction: **There are twenty-six new flavors at the ice cream shop.**

1.   The price of milk this week is three dollars and nine cents.

2.   Charles Lindbergh began his historic 2-day flight on May 20th, 1927, from Roosevelt Field, Long Island.

3.   Renting a bike on the island can cost more than $20.00 an hour.

4.   The local factory employs over three hundred people.

5.   Over the holidays, we saw four films, two plays, and 13 videos.

6.   Shop at the resale store and save over one-half off of department store prices.

7.   At the beginning of the 20th century, individuals traveled largely by horse; now we drive cars. What will we be doing at the end of the 21st century?

8.   The football game was a heartbreaker; the final score was Eagles six, Tigers seven.

9.   Our state budget is over 2,300,000,000 dollars.

10.   Set the alarm for five a.m. so that I am not late.

MECHANICS

4, Italics/Underlining   **Refer to the Handbook, pp. 216–218.**

Correct the following sentences by adding or removing italics as appropriate. Remember to indicate italics with continuous underlining (<u>such as this sample</u>).

For example: Have you read the new Stephen King novel, American Vampire?

Correction: Have you read the new Stephen King novel, <u>American Vampire?</u>

1.   Linda likes Microsoft Word, but I prefer WordPerfect.

2.   It is important to seek marriage counseling before you get married.

3.   I asked him to explain what noblesse oblige means.

4.   I read about all the flooding in the south in The Detroit News.

5.   Tina objected to Dickens's frequent use of a deus ex machina to resolve his fantastically-plotted novels.

6.   He invited Carlos to the parking lot to settle the matter mano a mano.

7.   James Fenimore Cooper's The Last of the Mohicans was made into a movie 166 years after its original publication.

8.   Keith Urban's new song, Til Summer Comes Around, is now the number one single in Canada.

9.   His class is reading Dante's Divine Comedy in parallel texts.

10. When we saw the Mona Lisa at The Louvre in France, we were surprised the painting was so small.

5, The Hyphen   **Refer to the Handbook, pp. 218–221.**

Correct the following sentences by either adding or removing hyphens as appropriate.

For example: This library program is only for two year olds.

Correction: This library program is only for two-year-olds.

1.   To avoid my ex husband, I never drive down Fifth Street.

2.   The ex Metropolitan Opera soprano joined our community chorus and improved the entire section's performance.

3.   The administration struggles to find new teachers before the start of the school-year.

4.   He was elected President of The Library Board by a vote of twenty one to sixteen.

5.   In pre revolutionary America, the colonists were subjects of the king of England.

6.   The police-officer told me that jaywalking was illegal in this town.

7.   Our neighbor Joe serves as the self appointed leader of the home-owners association.

8.   Our family hosted an eightieth birthday party for my greatgrandfather.

9.   The Chicago Museum of Natural History has an extensive collection of PreColumbian Art.

10.   From the eighteenth- to the twentieth-centuries, the West evolved from a pre industrial society to a post industrial one.

MECHANICS

6a, Basic Spelling Rules   **Refer to the Handbook, pp. 221–225.**

Correct the spelling errors in the following sentences by applying the basic spelling rules.

For example: Niether Jenny or Tom wants dessert.

Correction: **Neither Jenny nor Tom wants dessert.**

1. Ask the nieghbors if they would like to come over for grilled burgers and hot dogs.

2. Professor Guimard is very knowledgable about plate tectonics.

3. Lorraine was lying down thinking when an idea suddenly occured to her; half an hour later she had laid out all the fundamentals in the feild of astronomy.

4. Use your best judgement when selecting the vegetable plants.

5. You should recieve the check in the mail early next week.

6. Even after the surgery, the scar is barely noticable.

7. I love my brother, but I still think he's wierd.

8. The boy was couragous for jumping into the pond to save his younger brother.

9. It might sound odd, but our paper has two editor-in-chiefs.

10. The table setting and flower arrangement look lovly.

MECHANICS

6b, Words that Sound Alike   **Refer to the Handbook, pp. 225–226.**

The following sentences contain homophones used in error. Replace the incorrect word in each sentence with its correct sound-alike.

For example: I did not except the job offer because I cannot move to Chicago.

Correction: **I did not accept the job offer because I cannot move to Chicago.**

1.   As I walked up the mountain, I found myself gasping for breathe.

2.   In the 100-meter finals, Sarah was third and I was forth.

3.   Please chose a game piece.

4.   My teacher recommended that we always read the forward, as it usually defines the scope and approach of the book that follows.

5.   I prefer course ground pepper on my salad.

6.   When the passed president of the AFL-CIO addressed our school, he complemented the White House's new labor relations policy.

7.   Their should be enough chicken for everyone to have two pieces each.

8.   There are more apples on the trees then there were at this time last year.

9.   After four attempts, John finally past The Minnesota Bar Exam.

10.   Tie the boat to the peer and then join us in the restaurant.

IX RESEARCH WRITING

RESEARCH

Research exercises are incorporated into Section XI, MLA Style Documentation, and Format; Section XII, APA Style Documentation, and Format; and Section XIII, CMS Documentation and Format/CSE Documentation.

DISCPLINES

1a Understand Your Writing Assignment   **Refer to the Handbook, pp. 268–269.**

Using the following list of direction words, create a series of questions that will limit and focus the content of your paper. Select only the direction words that apply to the type of assignment. Refer to pp. 276–277 in your handbook for the meanings of the direction words.

Analyze

Argue

Categorize

Compare

Contrast

Critique

Define

Describe

Evaluate

Explain

Identify

Illustrate

Interpret

List

Outline

Prove

Review

Synthesize

Trace

**1b, e. Methods/Evidence and
Documentation/Format**   **Refer to the Handbook, pp. 270-272.**

Answer the following questions.

1. Define primary sources and give an example.

2. Define secondary sources and give an example.

3. Discuss the characteristics of an authoritative and reliable Internet source. Give an
   example of an authoritative and reliable Internet source for your discipline or paper topic.

4. What disciplines use the following documentation styles?

   a. MLA

   b. APA

   c. CMS

   d. CSE

5. What is the common feature of all four of the above mentioned documentation styles?

2d, Conventions for Writing about Literature   **Refer to the Handbook, pp. 283–285.**

The following brief piece about F. Scott Fitzgerald's short story "Bernice Bobs Her Hair" contains a number of violations of the conventions and suggestions contained in WRIT DISCIPLINES 2. Rewrite the piece making appropriate edits, and be prepared to discuss and explain your edits. Use MLA formatting conventions. (See Annotated Student Essay about Literature, pp. 287–289, in your Handbook.)

The 1920's: The Fashioning of a New Woman

F. Scott Fitzgerald's fourth short story to appear in the May 1, 1920 issue of "The Post," titled *Bernice Bobs Her Hair,* illustrated the angst young women face as they contemplated the question, "To bob or not to bob?" A bobbed hair cut was simply a short, straight cut level with the ears. Bobs took less time to wash, dry and style, so bobbed hair meant more leisure time for young women. But "compared to the long upswept hairstyles of the prior decade, the short bobs of the 1920's seemed masculine" {quote from Catherine Gourley's book "Flappers and the New American Woman" page 80}The new look, however, was not accepted by parents or much of 1920's society because it is considered a rebellious change in social norms. In Fitzgerald's story, *Bernice Bobs Her Hair,* the younger generation of women resists their mothers' social conventions, particularly the scrutinizing of young ladies' behavior at dances. The author describes the scene:

> "A great babel of middle-aged ladies with sharp eyes and icy hearts
> watched over the younger set and felt if they are not bombarded with stony
> eyes stray couples will dance weird barbaric interludes in the corner and
> the more popular, more dangerous girls, will sometimes be kissed in
> parked limousines of unsuspecting dowagers" {From Fitzgerald's *Bernice
> Bobs Her Hair pages 25-26)}.*

The story illustrates a new trend in the 1920's; younger women were beginning to seek more freedom to socialize with men without being under society's glare.

DISCIPLINES

2d, 3d, 4d, 5d
Conventions   Refer to the Handbook, pp. 276–278, 281, 285–286, 289–290.

Fill in the blanks in the following statements.

All Disciplines

1. Formal research writing in all of the disciplines avoids the _____ and _____ points of view.

Literature

2. When writing about literature, you can assume your readers already have read the piece of literature, so you can avoid _____.

3. When mentioning an author the first time within your paper, use the author's _____. After the first time, use _____.

4. Use the _____ tense when discussing works of literature. Use the _____ tense when referring to historical events, biographical material, or events prior to the time of the story's action.

Humanities

5. Investigators in the humanities rely heavily on _____ investigation in their research.

6. Researchers ask questions in order to _____, _____, or _____.

Social Sciences

7. Social sciences have their own technical language with specific meanings for words such as _____, _____, and _____.

8. Social scientists value _____ language and _____, _____, and _____ sentences in reporting their results.

Natural and Applied Sciences

9. Scientists make an effort to create a(n) _____ or _____ tone, preferring verbs that are _____ rather than _____.

10. Scientists include only information that enhances the reader's understanding of the _____, _____, and _____ of the experiment being discussed.

XI MLA–STYLE DOCUMENTATION AND FORMAT

MLA

Documentation and Format Questions   **Refer to the Handbook, Section XI.**

Respond to the following short answer questions.

1. What do the letters in the abbreviation MLA stand for?

2. What is the two-part system of documentation for MLA?

3. Why are in-text citations used in MLA-style documentation?

4. In most MLA in-text citations, what two elements of the source are included?

5. If you are citing a source with more than one author, how do you present the in-text citation?

6. If you are citing an electronic source, how do you present the in-text citation?

7. What is the list of sources in an MLA-style paper titled?

8. In what order are citations given in the list of sources in an MLA-style paper?

9. What are the formatting features of the list of sources in an MLA-style paper?

10. Describe the manuscript format for an MLA-style paper.

For each of the quotations provided, write an acceptable paraphrase and a paraphrase including a partial quotation that avoids plagiarism. Pay particular attention to the word choice and sentence structure of the original.

1. "The pile phenomenon might not exist except for a modern ailment known as *Information Anxiety*. This condition manifests as an unrealistic desire to keep up with the massive doses of information we're incessantly bombarded with nowadays." (Harriet Schechter's *Let Go Of Clutter*)

2. "Though Magdelaine might have felt excited and nervous about her marriage, she had grown up in a community that included fur traders, and surely knew that romance had little to do with Joseph LaFramboise's proposal of marriage. Marriage between traders and native families brought advantages for both husband and wife. It transformed the traders into family, friends, and allies within Indian communities, which depended heavily on fur trapping for their livelihood." (Virginia Law Burns' *Bold Women in Michigan History*)

3. "In 1856, laborer's working in a limestone quarry in the Neander Valley near Dusseldorf, Germany, dug up some unusual looking bones. Subsequent study revealed that they belonged to a previously unknown species of humans, similar to, but distinct from our own species, *Homo sapiens*. The newly discovered hominid was named Neandethal—*thal* is Old German for valley—and has fascinated anthropologists ever since." (Owen Edwards' Beyond *Bones*)

_____

_____

_____

_____

_____

4. "In his twenty-third year Abe left home for good and went out on his own. He helped build a flatboat and traveled down to New Orleans where he saw human beings bought and sold like cattle. Upon his return he settled in New Salem, working at odd jobs, cutting and splitting walnut fence rails to earn money for food and clothes. He helped out at store-keeping and quickly established the reputation for being "the cleverest fellow who ever broke into the establishment," a comment made by Jack Armstrong, the local strong-boy, after picking himself up off the ground where Abe had flung him." (Keith Jennison's *The Humorous Mr. Lincoln*)

_____

_____

_____

_____

_____

5. "For nearly a year and a half, the twenty-five men and one woman aboard the *Saint Anna* endured terrible hardships and danger as the icebound ship drifted helplessly north. Convinced the *Saint Anna* would never free herself from the ice, Albanov and thirteen crewmen left the ship in January 1914, hauling makeshift sledges and kayaks behind them across the frozen sea, hoping to reach the distant coast of Franz Josef Land. With only a shockingly inaccurate map to guide him, Albanov led his men on a 235-mile journey of continuous peril, enduring blizzards, disintegrating ice flows, attacks by polar bears and walrus, starvation, sickness, snow blindness, and mutiny." (Valerian Albanov's *The White Death*)

_____

_____

_____

_____

_____

6. "A person with outwardly expressive ADD will appear hyperactive both verbally and physically, be impulsive and outgoing, and will tend to take on more at one time than any ten people can accomplish. This type of person loves an audience; usually has a great sense of humor; and is dramatic, expressive, and very people-friendly. People with this type of ADD gravitate to sales, high-risk occupations, and the entertainments business, often becoming entrepreneurs." (Lynn Weiss' *A.D.D. on the Job*)

_____

_____

_____

_____

_____

7. "Southern leaders interpreted the events that culminated in secession in quite another way. Far from the South being aggressive, they insisted that the aggression was all on the other side. It was Northern violations of Southern rights—the aggressions of "Black Republicans"—that endangered the Union. Or so thought contemporary Southerners and some recent Southern historians as well." (Kenneth Stampp's *The Causes of the Civil War*)

_____

_____

_____

_____

_____

8. "Russia is neighbor to several Islamic states, former Soviet republics—whether one subscribes to a Huntingtonian thesis of civilization clashes or merely believes in civilization frictions, Russia occupies an unrivaled strategic position. Further, it occupies a strategic position in northeast Asia, particularly with regard to North Korea and China. As the noted Russian expert Dimitri Simes has repeatedly pointed out, Russian's geostrategic location places it in a unique position to exert influence on critical matters such as Iran's nuclear ambitions. An alliance with Russia is in our interest." (Viqi Wagner's (ed.) *Russia: Opposing Viewpoints*)

_____

_____

_____

_____

_____

9. "Over the past hundred years, the Pacific ocean warmed by almost four-fifths of a degree Celsius; and the land by about half a degree Celsius. The Arctic sea ice thinned by 40 percent. The warmer temperatures and drip of melting ice off the continents have expanded the volume of the sea, the newly enlarged waters overflowing into freshwater reservoirs, droning miles of coastline. The global sea level rose between ten and twenty centimeters during the past century." (Sonia Shah's *Crude*)

_____

_____

_____

_____

_____

10. "On the other hand, some folks say they no longer feel safe taking their families into the woods. Sportsmen complain too—bitterly. To many out West, where interior decorating tends to involve antlers and come fall, "howdy" is replaced by "Get your elk yet?" wolves are depicted as four-legged killing machines—land piranhas—ravaging game populations. Guys mutter about taking matters into their own hands and to hell with the feds. Bumper stickers show a crossed-out wolf and the slogan "Smoke a Pack a Day." (Douglas Chadwick's "Wolf Wars" in *National Geographic*)

_____

_____

_____

_____

_____

Integrating Borrowed Material   **Refer to the Handbook Section IX, pp. 258-261.**

Quotations are generally used to support and develop an idea already presented in your paper. For this exercise, first read the quotation provided and then develop a claim that can be supported and developed by the quotation. Second, briefly state your claim; and third, write a paragraph that employs all, or some, of the quotation provided to support and develop your claim.

Be sure to use a clear signal phrase (for example, using author name, authority, and selecting a precise and appropriate introductory verb such as "supports," "explains," "argues," etc.). Such signal phrases (1) help integrate the quotation smoothly into your own line of argument, (2) help your reader understand for what purpose the quotation is being used, and (3) help your reader distinguish your own thoughts from those of your quoted source.

For example:

Quotation and source: "Virtually all primary care providers prescribe Ritalin, but due to managed-care restraints, doctors complain that they cannot spend enough time with their patients." Stanley Turecki in *The Difficult Child, p.* 64.

Claim:

ADHD s a growing problem in our society, and we need to learn how to treat it effectively.

Paragraph incorporating quotation:

Very often when students are disruptive in the classroom and unable to sit quietly, they receive the label ADHD, *Attention-Deficit Hyperactivity Disorder.* Students may then be referred to the family physician for an assessment and possible drug therapy. According to Turecki, "virtually all primary care providers prescribe Ritalin, but due to managed-care restraints, doctors complain that they cannot spend enough time with their patients" (64). It is unlikely that a doctor who only spends a few minutes with the child can make an accurate diagnosis, one which often leads to prescribed medicine. In the best interest of the child, there should be a direct line of communication between teachers and doctors concerning the child's behavior.

1. Quotation and source: "Without beliefs, people would drift through life without anchor. Our beliefs are at the very heart of what makes us unique, what makes me "me" and you "you." They are directly linked to our ability to fully exploit our potential and find personal and professional happiness." Anna Rowley in *Leadership Therapy,* p. 41.

Claim:

_____

_____

Paragraph incorporating quotation:

_____

_____

_____

_____

_____

_____

_____

_____

_____

_____

_____

2. Quotation and source: "Becoming a credit card expert will also help you build a stronger FICO credit score. As far as I am concerned, your financial destiny goes nowhere without a good FICO credit score, yet I know many of you are not even aware of what a FICO credit score is, or the fact that you currently have three FICO credit scores that are playing a major role in your financial life." Suze Orman, in *Women and Money,* p. 89–90.

Claim:

_____

_____

Paragraph incorporating quotation:

_____

_____

_____

_____

_____

_____

_____

_____

_____

_____

3. Quotation and source: "When we look to how the Pilgrims and Wampanoags maintained more than fifty years of peace and how that peace suddenly erupted into one of the deadliest wars {King Philip's War} ever fought on American soil, the history of Plymouth Colony becomes something altogether new, rich, troubling, and complex.... The colonial forces ultimately triumphed, but at horrifying cost. By the end of the war, somewhere in the neighborhood of five thousand were dead with more than three-quarters of those losses suffered by the Native Americans." Nathaniel Philbrick in *Mayflower,* 2006, Preface, xii–xiii.

Claim:

_____

_____

Paragraph incorporating quotation:

_____

_____

_____

_____

_____

_____

_____

_____

_____

_____

For each of the following exercises, write a passage incorporating the quoted material and giving an MLA-style in-text citation. Use signal phrases as indicated.

For example:

  Format: Quote the following author using a signal phrase.

  Author: Stephen Hall

  Quote: "Since they became widely known in the 1920s, when commercial air travel was introduced between Lima and the southern Peruvian city of Arequipa, the mysterious desert drawings known as the Nasca lines have puzzled archaeologists, anthropologists, and anyone fascinated by ancient cultures in the Americas."

  Source: from *National Geographic* "Spirits in the Sand" March 29, 2010, p. 63

  Context: This is the only document by this author that is being used in the paper.

  Possible Answer:

  To explorers of cultural mysteries, Hall notes that "the mysterious desert drawings known as the Nasca lines have puzzled archaeologists, anthropologists, and anyone fascinated by ancient cultures in the Americas" (63).

1. Format: Quote the following author **without** using a signal phrase.

  Author: David Benioff

  Quote: "At last there were footsteps, several sets of heavy boots clomping in the corridor. A key turned in the lock. I sat up in bed and cracked my skull against the ceiling, hard enough that I bit through my lip.'"

  Source: *City of Thieves,* fiction, chapter 2, p. 39

Context: This is the only document by this author that is being used in the paper.

_____

_____

_____

_____

_____

2. Format: Quote the following author using a signal phrase.

   Author: David Benioff

   Quote: "At last there were footsteps, several sets of heavy boots clomping in the corridor. A key turned in the lock. I sat up in bed and cracked my skull against the ceiling, hard enough that I bit through my lip.'"

   Source: *City of Thieves,* fiction, chapter 2, p. 39

   Context: This is one of two documents by this author that is being used in the paper.

_____

_____

_____

_____

_____

3. Format: Quote the following authors **without** using a signal phrase.

   Authors: Michael Bloomberg and Joel Klein

   Quote: "The president wants to link billions of federal dollars to initiatives like ending the achievement gap between white and non-white students, evaluating teachers and awarding performance bonuses to principals and teachers who earn them."

   Source: *Time,* "Making the Grade" March 29, 2010, p. 49

   Context: This is the only document by these authors that is being used in this paper.

_____

_____

_____

_____

_____

4. Format: Quote the following authors using a signal phrase.

   Author(s): Michael Bloomberg and Joel Klein

   Quote: "The president wants to link billions of federal dollars to initiatives like ending the achievement gap between white and non-white students, evaluating teachers and awarding performance bonuses to principals and teachers who earn them."

   Source: *Time,* "Making the Grade" March 29, 2010, p. 49

   Context: This is one of three documents by these authors that is being used in this paper.

_____

_____

_____

_____

_____

5. Format: Quote the following author using a signal phrase.

   Author: Bill Streever

   Quote: "Water is strange stuff. Most substances, when cooled, contract. This is why thermometers work: mercury shrinks as it cools and expands as it warms. Warmth makes the molecules in a substance move faster. They dance around, bumping into one another. As the temperature increases, they dance faster, and when they bump into one another, they push harder. At thirty two degrees, the water starts to freeze… Newly frozen water is nine percent bigger than liquid water."

   Source: in *Cold,* September 2009, p. 34–35

   Context: This is one of two articles by this author that is being used in the paper.

   _____

   _____

   _____

   _____

   _____

6. Format: Quote the following author using a signal phrase.

   Author: Stuart Kallen

   Quote: "The *Catcher in the* Rye by J.D. Salinger has been described variously as extremely funny, tragic, uplifting, obscene, and as an American classic."

   Source: in *Understanding the Catcher in the Rye,* 2001, p. 8

   Context: This is the only piece by this author that is being used in the paper.

   _____

   _____

   _____

   _____

   _____

7. Format: Quote the following author using a signal phrase.

   Author: Anne Tierney

   Quote: "Computers have only very recently become common outside narrowly defined locations such as academia, business, and the military. We are just beginning to understand what the age of 'personal computing' will mean to our culture."

   Source: Personal Interview, 22 July 2001

   Context: This is the only document by this author that is being used in the paper.

_____

_____

_____

_____

8. Format: Quote the following authors **without** using a signal phrase.

  Authors: Corporate Author, The Staff of the Princeton Review

   Quote: "If you've ever studied a foreign language, you know what idioms are—and how much trouble they can be. An idiom is simply a peculiarity, a rule of usage that applies only to a particular instance."

   Source: *Grammar Smart,* 1998, p. 88

   Context: This is the only document by these authors that is being used in this paper.

_____

_____

_____

_____

9. Format: Quote the following authors using a signal phrase.

    Authors: Al Lindner, Fred Buller, Doug Stange, Dave Csanda, Ron Lindner, Bob Ripley & Jan Eggers

    Quote: "Even before the ice is off the lake and the first trickle of ice melt begins to run, the fish begin abandoning their winter haunts and start migrating toward and staging near their prospective spawning sites."

    Source: *Pike,* 1997, pp. 35–40

    Context: This is one of three documents by these authors that is being used in this paper.

_____

_____

_____

_____

_____

10. Format: Quote the following author using a signal phrase.

    Author(s): Editor, Donald Haase

    Quote: "Despite the efforts of the occupying military forces to strip away from German culture a text that they considered to have exerted a profoundly destructive influence on the German spirit, The Grimms' tales returned immediately to bookstore shelves."

    Source: *The Reception of Grimms' Fairy Tales,* 1993, p. 92

    Context: This is the only document by this author that is being used in the paper.

_____

_____

_____

_____

_____

A page of a student paper that should follow MLA guidelines appears on the next page. Lettered line segments mark a number of elements on the page. Complete the following list by indicating next to each letter the appropriate margin, position, or spacing. The first one is done for you as an example.

There are eleven additional formatting flaws in this sample page. List them and describe what should have been done instead. Use the spaces provided.

    (a) <u>top of page</u> to <u>last name/page number</u>: 1/2 inch

1.   **(b)**   top and bottom margins:

2.   **(c)**   line spacing:

3.   **(d)**   left margin:

4.   **(e)**   right margin:

5.   **(f)** _____

6.   **(g)** _____

7.   **(h)** _____

8.   **(i)** _____

9.   **(j)** _____

10.   **(k)** _____

11.   **(l)** _____

(b)

(a)

Lorem ipsum dolor sit amet, consectetuer adipiscing

(c) **(g)** Elit, sed diam nonummy nibh euismod tincidunt ut laoreet
Dolore magna aliquam erat volutpat.

(h) **MAJOR HEADING**

Duis autem vel eum irirure dolor in hendrerit in vulpputate
velit esse molestie consequat, abitando quest'anno in
toscano. Vel ilium doloreeu feugiat nulla facilisis at
vero eros et accumsan – iusto odio dignissim qui
blandit.

(e)

(d)(j)

(i) **Subheading**

Ut wisi enim ad minim veniam, quis nostrud exerci tation
ullamcorper suscipit lobortis nisl ut aliquip ex ea
commodo consequat, Duis autem vel eum iriure dolor in
hendrerit in vulputate velit esse moletie; consequat,
vel illum dolore eu feugiat nulla facilisis at veto eros
et accumsan et iusto odio dignissim qui blandit praesent
luptatum:

> **(k)** "Delenit augue duis dolore te feugait nulla
> facilisi. Lorem ipsum dolor sit amet,
> consdectetuer adipscing elit, sed...nonummy
> aliquam erat volutpat. Ut wisi eniom ad minim
> veniam, quis nostrud aliquip ex ea commodo
> consequat." **(l)**

Duis autem vel eum iriure dolor in hendrerit in vulputate
velit esse molestie consequat, vel illum dolore eu

(b)

Using the following sources, create a works cited page in MLA format.

1. **Article Title:** Attention-deficit hyperactivity disorder outcomes for children treated in community-based pediatric settings. (Journal Article)
    Author: Jeffery Epstein, et al.
    Journal: Archives of Pediatrics & Adolescent Medicine. Vol 164, issue #2, in January 2010. begins on p. 15 and continues for 11 pages
    Found in: Expanded Academic Index in Info Trac database on March 25, 2010

2. **Article Title:** Information needs of parents of children with attention-deficit disorder (Journal Article)
    Author: Emma Sciberras, et al.
    Journal: Clinical Pediatrics, January 2010. No pages given
    Found in: Expanded Academic Index in Info Trac database on March 25, 2010

3. **Article Title:** Attention-deficit hyperactivity disorder: recent advances in pediatric pharmacotherapy (Journal Article)
    Author: Diane E. May and Christopher J. Kratochvil (Journal Article)
    Journal: Drugs fall 2010, vol 70, issue #1. Begins on p. 15 and continues for 4 pages
    Found in: Expanded Academic Index in Info Trac database on March 25, 2010

4. **Book Title:** The Autism & ADHD Diet
    Edited by: Barrie Silerberg
    Publisher: Sourcebooks, Inc. in Naperville, Illinois
    Copyright: 2000

5. **Book Title:** The Difficult Child
    Author: Stanley Turecki
    Publisher: Bantam Books in New York
    Copyright: 2000

6. Attention-Deficit Hyperactivity Disorder Found on website NIHM (National Institute of Mental Health) http://www.nimh.nih.gov/health/publications/attention-deficit-hyperactivity-disorder on March 25, 2010

7. New Gene Linked to ADHD can be found at http://www.webmd.com/add-adhd/default.htm on March 25, 2010

XII APA–STYLE DOCUMENTATION
AND FORMAT

APA

Documentation and Format Questions   **Refer to the Handbook, Section XII.**

Respond to the following short answer questions.

1. What do the letters in the abbreviation APA stand for?

2. What is the two-part system of documentation for APA?

3. Why are in-text citations used in APA-style documentation?

4. In most APA in-text citations, what two elements of the source are included?

5. If you are citing a source with more than one author, how do you present the in-text citation?

6. If you are citing an electronic source, how do you present the in-text citation?

7. What is the list of sources in an APA-style paper titled?

8. In what order are citations given in the list of sources in an APA-style paper?

9. What are the formatting features of the list of sources in an APA-style paper?

10. Describe the manuscript format for an APA-style paper.

2, APA Manuscript Format   **Refer to the Handbook, pp. 340-343.**

A page of a student paper that should follow APA guidelines appears on the next page. Lettered line segments mark a number of elements on the page. Complete the following list by indicating next to each letter the appropriate margin, position, or spacing. The first one is done for you as an example.

In addition, there are eleven formatting flaws in this sample page. List them and describe what should have been done instead. Use the spaces provided.

   (a) <u>top of page</u> to <u>last name/page number:</u> 1/2inch

1. **(b)** top and bottom margins:

2. **(c)** line spacing:

3. **(d)** left margin:

4. **(e)** right margin:

5. **(f)** _____

6. **(g)** _____

7. **(h)** _____

8. **(i)** _____

9. **(j)** _____

10. **(k)** _____

11. **(l)** _____

(a)
(f)

(b)

Smith page 3

(c) Lorem ipsum dolor sit amet, Consectetuer adipiscing elit, sed

diam nonummy Nibh euismod tincidunt ut laoreet dolore magna

aliquam erat volutpat.

MAJOR HEADING **(k)**

(h) Duis autem vel eum irirure dolor in hendrerit in vulpputate
velit esse molestie consequat, abitando quest'anno in
toscano. Vel ilium doloreeu feugiat nulla facilisis at
vero eros et accumsan – iusto odio dignissim qui blandit.

(e)

(d)

Subheading **(l)**

Ut wisi enim ad minim veniam, quis nostrud exerci tation
ullamcorper suscipit lobortis nisl ut aliquip ex ea commodo
consequat, Duis autem vel eum iriure dolor in hendrerit in
vulputate velit esse moletie; consequat, vel illum dolore eu
feugiat nulla facilisis at veto eros et accumsan et iusto odio
dignissim qui blandit praesent luptatum:

(i) "Delenit augue duis dolore te feugait nulla
facilisi. Lorem ipsum dolor sit amet,
consdectetuer adipscing elit, sed...nonummy
aliquam erat volutpat. Ut wisi eniom ad minim
veniam, quis nostrud aliquip ex ea commodo
consequat." **(j)**

(g)
Duis autem vel eum iriure dolor in hendrerit in vulputate
velit esse molestie consequat, vel illum dolore Vel illum
dolore eu feugiat nulla facilisis at veto eros et accumsar,
et iusto odio dignissim qui blandit.

(b)

120

Using the following sources, create a reference page in APA format.

1. **Author**: Victor Papanek
   Title: The Green Imperative
   Place of Publication: New York
   Publisher: Thames and Hudson, Inc.
   Date of publication: 1995
   Number of pages: 256 pages

2. **Author:** J.L. Kennedy
   Article Title: Alternative Energy, Climate Change Proposals Debated
   Title: Pennsylvania Law Weekly
   Date of Publication: March 9, 2010 Vol. 3 Issue 12
   Page number: 79–84
   Retrieved from: Expanded Index. Info Trac.

3. **Authors:** Kari Foster, Debbie Hindman, and Annette Stelmack
   Title: Sustainable Residential Interiors
   Place of Publication: Hoboken, New Jersey
   Publisher: John Wiley & Sons, Inc.
   Date of Publication: 2007

4. **Author**: John Carlton
   Title: Solar Panels Generate Energy and Arguments
   Journal Title: Wall Street Journal Online
   Date of Publication: 2009 no volume or page numbers given
   Web Address: http://www.realestatejournal.com/homegarden/20040608-carlton.html

5. **Author**: Matthew Phillips
   Title: A Major Alternative-Energy Moment in Texas
   Title of Magazine: Newsweek
   Date of Publication: March 29, 2010 vol. 147 iss. 13
   Page numbers: 23-30

6. **Author**: Unknown
   Title: Recent State Actions Promoting Alternative Energy
   Date: Retrieved March 25, 2010
   Web address: http://www.nga.or/center.com

7. **Author**: Arthur Tiller
    Title: New Sources of Alternative Energy
    Title of Magazine: Environmental News
    Date of Publication: Jan. /Feb. 2009
    Reprinted in: Advances in Environmental Science
    Editor: David Mc Mann
    Place of Publication: New York
    Publisher: Preston Press
    Date of Publication: 2010
    Pages: 22–32

XIII CMS DOCUMENTATION AND FORMAT
CSE DOCUMENTATION

CMS

Documentation and Format Questions   **Refer to the Handbook, pp. 351–364.**

Respond to the following short answer questions.

1. What do the letters in the abbreviation CMS stand for?

2. What is the two-part system of documentation for CMS?

3. Why are endnotes used in CMS documentation?

4. The first time a source is cited in CMS, what elements of the source are included?

5. If you are citing a source with more than one author, how do you present the endnote?

6. If you are citing an electronic source, how do you present the endnote?

7. What is the list of sources in a CMS paper titled?

8. In what order are citations given in the list of sources in a CMS paper?

9. What are the formatting features of the list of sources in a CMS paper?

10. Describe the manuscript format for a CMS paper.

Using the following sources, create a bibliography page in CMS format.

1. **Editor:** Keith W. Jennison
   Title: The Humorous Mr. Lincoln (Book)
   Place of Publication: New York, NY
   Publisher: Bantam Books
   Date of Publication: 1965

2. **Author:** Arthur Peters
   Title: Seven Trails West (Book)
   Place of Publication: New York, NY
   Publisher: Abbeville Press
   Date of Publication: 1996

3. **Author:** William Marvell
   Article Title: Staying the Course at Gettysburg (Magazine)
   Title: Civil War Times
   Date of Publication: April 2010
   Page numbers: 40

4. **Authors:** Thomas Craughwell
   Article Title: Stealing Lincoln's Body
   Title: Journal of the Abraham Lincoln Association (Online Journal)
   Date of Publication: Winter 2008 volume 29 no. 1
   Date Retrieved: Accessed March 25, 2010
   Web address: http://historycooperative.org/journals/jala/29.1/index.html
   Page numbers: 79–87

5. **Author:** Edward Rothstein
   Article Title: Reconsidering the Man From Illinois (Newspaper Article)
   Title: New York Times
   Date of Publication: December 11, 2008
   Page numbers: not given; Arts section, Midwest edition

6. **Author:** Tyler Anbinder
   Article Title: Which Poor Man's Fight? Immigrants and the
   Federal Conscription of 1863 (Article from Online Subscription Database)
   Title: Civil War History
   Date of Publication: December 2006 volume 52 issue 4
   Page numbers: 344 (29)
   Database: Expanded Academic Index in InfoTrac database
   Retrieved Date: March 15, 2007
   Web Address: http://80-find.galegroup.com.ezproxy.falcon.edu/itx/basicSearch

Respond to the following short answer questions.

1. What do the letters in the abbreviation CSE stand for?

2. What is the two-part system of documentation for CSE?

3. What are the three different systems for referring to a reference within a paper in CSE-style documentation?

4. If you are citing a source with more than one author, how do you present the in-text citation using the name-year system?

5. What is the list of sources in a CSE-style paper titled?

6. If you use the citation-sequence system for your in-text citations, in what order are citations given in the list of sources in a CSE-style paper?

7. If you use the name-year system for your in-text citations, in what order are citations given in the list of sources in a CSE-style paper?

8. If you use the citation-name system for your in-text citations, in what order are citations given in the list of sources in a CSE-style paper?

9. What are the formatting features of the list of sources in a CSE-style paper?

10. If you use the CSE citation-name system, describe the process for preparing both in-text and list of sources citations.

Using the following sources, create a references page in CSE format.

1. **Author:** N.H. Nguyen, C.P. McPhee, and C.M. Wade
    Article Title: Genetic Variation and Responses in Reproductive Performance of Sows
    Title: Animal Science (Online Journal)
    Date of Publication: February 2006 volume 82 issue 1
    Page numbers: 7–12
    Retrieved Date: March 25, 2010
    Web Address: http://www.journals.cambridge.org

2. **Author:** T. Jones, Compiler
    Title: 2008 IUCN Red List of Threatened Species
    Date of Publication: 2008
    Retrieved Date: March 25, 2010
    Web Address: http://www.iucnredlist.org

3. **Author:** P. S. Hentz
    Title: Rescuing Wildlife: A Guide to Helping Injured and Orphaned Animals
    Place of Publication: Mechanicsburg, PA
    Publisher: Stackpole Books
    Date of Publication: 2009
    Number of Pages: 130

4. **Editors:** E. D. Norse, L.G. Crowder, and M.C. Soule
    Title: Marine Conservation Biology (Book with Editors)
    Place of Publication: New York, NY
    Publisher: Island Press
    Date of Publication: 2005
    Number of Pages: 496

5. **Author:** W.P. Yardley
    Article Title: Wolves Aren't Making it Easy on Idaho Hunters
    Title: New York Times (Newspaper)
    Date of Publication: September 10, 2009
    Pages: Section A12

6. **Authors:** A. Lopez, R. Alkemade, and P.A. Verweij
    Article Title: The Impacts of Roads and Other Infrastructure on Mammal and Bird Populations: A Meta-Analysis
    Title: Biological Conservation (Journal)
    Date of Publication: 2010 volume 143 issue 4
    Pages: 825–1034

XIV ESL BASICS

AN IMPORTANT REMINDER FOR STUDENTS: Because of the flexibility of the English language, there may be more than one way to correct the errors in each exercise. This is particularly true in this section. If you have any questions about your answers versus the ones supplied in the Selected Answers section, please ask your instructor. Very likely there will be other students with the same or similar questions.

ESL

1a, Modals   **Refer to the Handbook, pp. 377–378.**

Correct the use of modal auxiliaries in the following sentences.

For example: The students will not to use the new computers.

Correction: **The students will not use the new computers.**

1.   By the end of the day, John be done weeding the garden.

2.   Next season's team will to play soccer on the football field.

3.   Do you think you should will visit us this summer in Florida?

4.   Because Lily is grounded, she cannot to play with us in the park.

5.   When I was growing up, my family will usually take a trip in the summer.

6.   Elly is knowing how to operate the slide projector.

7.   When Jesse finally finishes his degree he be happy.

8.   The new boy can plays the violin very well.

9.   I can have to leave early.

10.   He must practicing his drum solo all night.

1b, Perfect Tenses   **Refer to the Handbook, pp. 378–379.**

Correct the use of perfect tenses in the following sentences.

For example: The doctor have decided to retire next year.

Correction: **The doctor has decided to retire next year.**

1. My aunts have make over three thousand pieces of bead jewelry.

2. The football players has eating all day.

3. Bill goes to the movies frequently; he will have saw the latest comedy already.

4. Chloë had sang in the choir for three years before she was chosen to be its director.

5. Suzanne have flew into Detroit over three times in the last year.

6. The credit card companies has raised interest rates again.

7. As of next spring, our organization will had support the children's hospital for twenty-five years.

8. I have wrote Senator Joe Jones and asked him not to vote to increase my taxes.

9. Uncle Ken and Aunt Kelly has been gone for over an hour.

10. The chef at the new restaurant have created a new dessert every week.

1c, Progressive Tenses   Refer to the Handbook, pp. 379–381.

Correct the use of progressive tenses in the following sentences.

For example: The baby been sleeping for over six hours.

Correction: **The baby has been sleeping for over six hours.**

1.   John seeing Reno for the first time.

2.   The college are giving away free textbooks.

3.   The ozone layer been thinning because of the release of harmful chemicals.

4.   My boss is being unhappy because I arrived late to work today and missed the meeting.

5.   Sanga had be thinking calculus was easy until he took the midterm exam.

6.   My neighbor Joe is run for state representative this year.

7.   They will working on the scenery this afternoon.

8.   By the time Mr. Tottle retires next year, he will been teaching at NBHS for thirty-eight years.

9.   The girls be dancing to the new Chris Brown song.

10.   Julia been crying ever since her boyfriend left for the Army.

1d, Passive Voice 1   **Refer to the Handbook, pp. 381–382.**

Correct the use of the passive voice in the following sentences.

For example: The older woman was helped out of the burning building by the firefighter.

Correction: **The older woman was helped out of the burning building by the firefighter.**

1.   The NBA championship was winned by San Antonio this year.

2.   The national anthem is play before every hockey game.

3.   We could not believe we were sitted next to the president of the United States.

4.   Many instructions now is written in both English and Spanish.

5.   Every student are expected to do well in his or her studies.

6.   Most of the trout is catch by beginning fishermen.

7.   Ms. Harris were speechless when she won first place.

8.   The book were wrote by an anonymous author.

9.   My pants were burnt when I ironed with the temperature too high.

10.   The barn owl were eating a lot of field mice.

1d, Passive Voice 2 **Refer to the Handbook, pp. 381–382.**

Rewrite the following passive voice sentences in the active voice.

For example: My editorial was read by everyone in my office.

Correction: **Everyone in my office read my editorial.**

1. My backpack was lost yesterday by Terusuke.

2. Lip gloss is worn by many young women.

3. *Carmen* was written by Bizet.

4. Many citizens are angered by the new tax on cigarettes.

5. The books were saved by the library staff.

6. A good time was had by everyone.

7. Affordable housing was spoken about by the Birmingham City Council at every meeting.

8. The satellite was boosted into orbit by the shuttle *Endeavor.*

9. The people at our table were pleased with the flaming soufflé.

10. *Oliver Twist* was written by Charles Dickens.

1e, Two-Word Verbs   Refer to the Handbook, pp. 382–383.

Correct the two-word verbs in the following sentences.

For example: Phil came a helpful article across.

Correction: Phil came across a helpful article.

1. Where's the newspaper? Oh, John threw away it.

2. The police officer helped the motorist out after the accident.

3. Because of the extensive fire damage, the fire marshal ordered the building's owners to tear down it.

4. The survivors clung the boat to.

5. Why doesn't he pick someone on his own size?

6. My grandmother let me sleep last night over.

7. When you are in Santa Fe, don't forget to look up me.

8. Your book is overdue; please turn in it soon.

9. If you do not think he is offering a fair price, turn the offer down.

10. My dad learned that smoking was unhealthy, so he gave up it.

1f, Verbals   **Refer to the Handbook, pp. 383-385.**

Correct the verbals in the following sentences.

For example: His father cautioned him using the crosswalk always.

Correction: His father cautioned him always to use the crosswalk.

    OR: His father cautioned him about always using the crosswalk.

1.   They agreed come over here before the game.

2.   Josef misses himself to eat home-cooked meals.

3.   My personal trainer helped to take off ten pounds in two weeks.

4.   My brother thinks to act is an exciting profession.

5.   When I finish to eat, I'll read to you.

6.   We should be to help the food kitchen this time of year.

7.   Eriq is beginning sounding good on the piano.

8.   Sam should learn eating a healthy diet.

9.   Otto's parents invited me come with them to the show.

10.   We thought to visit the home of George Washington would be a perfect ending to our trip.

2a–c, Count and Noncount Nouns 1   Refer to the Handbook, pp. 386–387.

Correct the use of count and noncount nouns in the following sentences.

For example: The chef put too much salts in the soup.

Correction: The chef put too much salt in the soup.

1.   Gordon knows many local history.

2.   How many breads do you need for your dinner party?

3.   Please empty the sands out of your shoes before you get into the car.

4.   Guadalupe said much machines are built there.

5.   How many pieces of fishes do you think the boys will eat?

6.   Our county had a record amount of snows this year.

7.   My car used only 7 gallons of gasolines for the 300-mile trip.

8.   Your vehicle registration card is an information you should always have in your car.

9.   The United States mixes much cultures.

10.   The baby already weights fourteen pound!

2a–b, Count and Noncount Nouns 2   Refer to the Handbook, pp. 386–387.

Correct the use of count and noncount nouns in the following sentences.

For example: The store's antique furnitures are quite expensive.

Correction: **The store's antique furniture is quite expensive.**

1.   Gianni lost his cashes through a hole in his pocket.

2.   Do you have enough quarter for the vending machine?

3.   How much people's will be at the wedding shower?

4.   Is Karen still looking for the place to live?

5.   You have my full confidences.

6.   How many rain fell here last month?

7.   How many book will you need to purchase this semester?

8.   Cook the eggs for ten to fifteen minute.

9.   There is not much times before our mid-term exam.

10.   Try to fit all twenty table in the banquet hall.

2c–d, Articles   Refer to the Handbook, pp. 387–389.

Correct the use of articles (definite, indefinite) in the following sentences. In some instances, the correction may involve deleting the article.

For example: Do not sell until you have the great offer.

Correction: Do not sell until you have a great offer.

1.   Hour ago he left for the office.

2.   A first assignment is to read chapter one of a classroom textbook.

3.   When she finishes the high school, she wants to travel before finding an employment.

4.   It is an short trip to the coast.

5.   George tried many odd jobs before joining a Navy.

6.   Please pick me up pound of the coffee when you're at the market.

7.   Michael Buble not only sings, but he also plays a piano.

8.   Vietnam War still seems very recent to me.

9.   The Honorable Judge Hotalling presided at hearing.

10.   My birthday is a best day of the year.

2d, Definite Article Refer to the Handbook, pp. 388-389.

Correct the use of the definite article in the following sentences.

For example: My husband is from St. Louis area.

Correction: My husband is from the St. Louis area.

1. Please pass some ketchup.

2. Highway 62 is easiest way to get to the amusement park.

3. We saw young man who was elected Mayor of Hamburg.

4. The hockey is very popular here.

5. I saw the Bob walking down the hall just a minute ago.

6. Kelly wakes early every morning to get to the work on time.

7. After graduating, Francine was hired by the NASA.

8. My son is searching for best college in Michigan.

9. I read last week that the calcium is important in a diet.

10. Traverse City is "Cherry Capital of the World."

3a, Cumulative Adjectives   **Refer to the Handbook, pp. 389–390.**

Correct the word order of the adjectives in the following items.

For example: his new first tooth

Correction: his first new tooth

1.   a brown big bear

2.   my new first bicycle

3.   round small stones

4.   a brick ancient fireplace

5.   triangular large seven windows

6.   the green small plant

7.   a wooden white fence

8.   the German most knowledgeable scientist

9.   some small older cabs

10.   the ten top albums of the year

3b, Present and Past Participles   **Refer to the Handbook, pp. 390.**

Correct the following sentences by changing past and present participles as necessary.

For example: Lying on the beach is always relaxed.

Correction: Lying on the beach is always relaxing.

1.   Running is energized.

2.   The winter winds here are very dried.

3.   She found the doctor's demeanor troubled.

4.   Jackie's remarks annoying me.

5.   The new horror movie is frightened.

6.   Many visitors find the highways around Los Angeles confused.

7.   Devin's constant corny jokes annoying me.

8.   Jean saw depressed similarities in the history of the 1930s and the 1990s.

9.   I found Pacino's performance engaged.

10.   After losing our luggage and sleeping under a leaking roof, we regretting our trip.

3c, Adverbs   Refer to the Handbook, pp. 390-391.

Correct the placement of adverbs in the following sentences.

For example: My teenage sons always are hungry.

Correction: My teenage sons are always hungry.

1.   The toddler ate quickly his cereal.

2.   There seems never to be enough time.

3.   My new neighbor always is in a hurry.

4.   I drove enough fast to get to work on time.

5.   When we visit New Orleans, we eat typically at Le Meritage Inn.

6.   Peter gave happily his present to his mother.

7.   After working in the yard all day, I was enough sleepy to go to bed early.

8.   Tell your children to never talk to strangers.

9.   John mailed early his package.

10.   When Kyle asked Sue to marry him, she was happy extremely.

Correct the use of prepositions in the following sentences. The correction may include removing prepositions as well as adding them.

For example: I read about the fall festival on the newspaper.

Correction: **I read about the fall festival in the newspaper.**

1. I went the movies nearly every week last summer.

2. Put the clean laundry in the bed.

3. When we first moved at Toronto, I missed Hong Kong very much.

4. The best place to look for shoes is on the new shopping mall.

5. After his trip in Somalia, the landscape in New England looked at very green to him.

6. Ask the woman who works over the deli what lunchmeat is on sale this week.

7. Though I had read Shakespeare in translation before coming to the States, I am finding it entirely new for English.

8. The downtown bus stops at here at quarter past and quarter of the hour.

9. The couple was married over the gazebo.

10. When you go the store today, pick up some fresh fish.

Correct the use of prepositions in the following sentences. The correction may include removing prepositions as well as adding them.

For example: When we informed the landlord on the problem, he promised to fix it.

Correction: **When we informed the landlord of the problem, he promised to fix it.**

1.   I was not accustom of wearing my new glasses.

2.   My brother's new glasses are for to read.

3.   The movie *Precious* was based in the novel *Push* by Sapphire.

4.   Four quarters is equal of one dollar.

5.   I like to paint as to well draw.

6.   Because their team ran the relay in record time, they qualified in the final race.

7.   "Come along me," called Gisela to Dave.

8.   If you are not satisfied in your new plants, you may return them for your money back.

9.   Addition to this book, you'll need that one.

10.   Would you be interested of purchasing popcorn from my Girl Scout troop?

5a–b, Omitted Verbs and Subjects   **Refer to the Handbook, pp. 394.**

Correct the following sentences by ensuring that each clause has one subject and that linking verbs are present when needed.

For example: The school has twenty-two bus runs a day. Will have twenty-seven bus runs next year.

Correction: **The school has twenty-two bus runs a day, but the school will have twenty-seven bus runs next year.**

1.   My younger brother, who is a professional trumpet player, he travels around the world and plays for his fans.

2.   Dirk's whole family very amusing.

3.   All my new flowers, they died after last night's frost.

4.   Today's speaker very dry and boring.

5.   The crickets in the trees in my neighborhood they sing all day.

6.   If clichés not true, why are they so often repeated?

7.   Aunt Millie's famous apple pie, the one that won the blue ribbon at the state fair, it is best served with vanilla ice cream.

8.   Dan's notebook, containing all his laboratory notes, it has been missing since yesterday.

9.   My black lab Buster, who has been swimming in the river, he tracked in mud all over the house.

10.   We visited Chicago three times this year. Visited three times last year, too.

5c, Expletives   Refer to the Handbook, pp. 394–395.

Correct the use of expletives and verb agreement in the following sentences.

For example: Is a gorgeous rose bush.

Correction: **It is a gorgeous rose bush.**

1.   There is three interstate highways into downtown Atlanta.

2.   There is three drawings before the grand prize give away.

3.   Here is all the flowers you ordered from the florist.

4.   Is only three days until my birthday.

5.   There is many volunteers who are willing to work all night.

6.   Though the park is crowded, is still fun to be here.

7.   I wish there was another sale on bathing suits.

8.   There is three stores on my block.

9.   Is always a good idea to eat before we go to the grocery store.

10.   Is true he won't run for another term as mayor?

6b, Questions with *Who*, *Whom*, and *What*   Refer to the Handbook, pp. 396–397.

Correct the word order and helping verbs in the following questions containing *who*, *whom*, and *what*.

For example: What eggs to hatch happens after?

Correction: **What happens after the eggs hatch?**

  1.   Do James want to eat dinner with us tonight?

  2.   Whom created the congressional gridlock?

  3.   Whom the instructor choose to go first?

  4.   Who today's mail brings in?

  5.   What the team does?

  6.   Who is believing that explanation?

  7.   To who they sent the package?

  8.   What tides and currents in the ocean create?

  9.   Who sleep in the tent tonight?

  10.   What sandwich John wants for lunch?

6c, Indirect Questions 1   **Refer to the Handbook, pp. 397.**

For each sentence, find the indirect question and rewrite it as a direct question.

For example: I am not sure how much food to prepare.

Answer: **How much food should I prepare?**

1.   The team wondered how much the new building and cafeteria would cost.

2.   He thought he knew which astronomer first identified black holes.

3.   I'm not sure why we are all here.

4.   He knew which child he should keep an eye on.

5.   Gena wonders how the U.S. Congress differs from the British Parliament.

6.   I wasn't sure our new boss allowed a four day work week.

7.   The engineers investigated how gravity affected the growth of crystals.

8.   Robert didn't know when we could visit the Dow Planetarium in Montreal.

9.   I am searching for a solution to rid my garden of Asian beetles.

10.   My husband asked me what I would wear to his high school reunion.

6c, Indirect Questions 2   **Refer to the Handbook, pp. 397.**

Correct the following indirect questions by using proper word order and verbs.

For example: The lead story traced how has drug use changed in the last decade.

Correction: **The lead story traced how drug use has changed in the last decade.**

1.   My sister asked me will you be my maid of honor or not.

2.   My brother wasn't sure when did I get so smart.

3.   I tried to see where did my keys go.

4.   The committee researched why has the cost of education outpaced inflation in the last ten years.

5.   The server asked do you plan on eating on the deck.

6.   The reporter asked when will we see the mayor's new budget.

7.   Explain how does this machine work.

8.   My nephew wondered did I want to go to the park with him.

9.   Our instructor not sure we can complete the project before the end of the semester.

10.   Dave asked himself how can I date a woman who is never on time?

6d, Reported Speech   Refer to the Handbook, pp. 397–399.

For the following sentences, rewrite the direct quotations as reported speech and the reported speech as direct quotation.

Reported: She said that St. Louis is her favorite city to visit in the summer.

Direct: She said, "St. Louise is my favorite city to visit in the summer."

Direct: "How can you get your homework finished," asked my mother, "when you stay out until midnight?"

Reported: My mother asked how I could get my homework finished when I stayed out until midnight.

1.   "I love zucchini," said Nino, "almost as much as I love peppers."

2.   The librarian told me that the new book I wanted was already checked out.

3.   "Roger has played cello in a faltering but passionate way for years," Erin stated with a grin.

4.   The president of the company announced that there would be severe layoffs this summer.

5.   "Wait for the third-quarter results," said the company spokesperson.

6.   The foreign exchange student observed that people in the United States dressed informally.

7.   "Will the economy improve this year, Mr. Bernanke?" the anxious Senate Finance Committee member asked.

8.   My therapist asked how long I have had pain in my knee.

9.   "Will you and your family be willing to work in the food kitchen again this year?" Mr. Jones asked.

10.   Whenever my grandmother found me working late, she would tell me that two hours at night were worth one hour in the morning.

6e, Conditional Sentences   Refer to the Handbook, pp. 399-401.

Correct the verbs in the following conditional sentences.

For example: If you eat right, you will be staying healthy.

Correction: **If you eat right, you will stay healthy.**

1.   If he sees a shooting star, he will make a wish.

2.   If you train harder, you could make the team.

3.   If I had a better boss, I may have been manager by now.

4.   Wherever Fleetwood Mac performed last year, they find big audiences.

5.   If you could go anywhere on vacation, where will you go?

6.   If you were the laboratory's teaching assistant, what will you do?

7.   Whenever she has trouble sleeping, she will drink some warm milk and go right back to bed.

8.   If we stop for lunch before going back to work, we would not have to interrupt our afternoon.

9.   When I exercise at least three days per week, my back will never bother me.

10.   Until you tell me to stop borrowing your clothes, I am assuming you do not mind.

XV GLOSSARY OF USAGE

Glossary

Usage 1   **Refer to the Handbook, pp. 403–411.**

Correct the errors in word usage in the following sentences.

Example: Jerry wins a award every year for his writing.

Answer: **Jerry wins an award every year for his writing.**

1. We can't leave without Kevin, and he ain't anywhere in the building.

2. The reason Nicholas loved music of all types is because he was in a music appreciation class.

3. You should of known ever person at the party.

4. What are the affects of smoking?

5. Jason can't hardly get his work done because of school.

6. Is your dinner alright?

7. The traffic was so light that we had no problem getting their on time.

8. Who's shoes are on the picnic table?

9. The ozone layer has decreased alot in the past twenty years.

10. I can't hardly wait for my twenty-first birthday.

11. Second hand smoke can effect all of us.

12. I am anxious to see my best friend again.

13. I can't decide between the chocolate cake, the apple pie, or the vanilla ice cream.

14. Hopefully, he past this class.

15. She was suppose to stay with the group, but she wandered away from it.

GLOSSARY

Usage 2   Refer to the Handbook, pp. 403–411.

Replace the italicized word—used incorrectly—in each of the following sentences with the correct word. Then identify the part of speech and write a short definition for both the incorrect and correct words. Consult a dictionary if necessary.

Example: Mr. Kinney is the *principle* of our school.

Answer: Mr. Kinney is the principal of our school.

principal(noun): leader

principle (noun): truth or basic assumption

principal (adj): first or foremost

1. What are the *affects* of the new spending bill?

2. It is important that everyone at the meeting remain *civic*.

3. Emile *can't hardly* read without going to sleep.

4. *Irregardless* of the time it takes to complete the project, you will receive six-thousand dollars.

5. Try to keep Mr. Kessler from going off on a *tangible*.

6. We will *loose* the contest if the judge finds our parents helped us with our project.

7. The extra isolation in the walls and ceiling help to keep down our heating cost.

8. Please *lie* the clean clothes on my bed.

9. The facilitator successfully *meditated* the dispute.

10. There is *fewer* salt in this shaker than the others.

SELECTED ANSWERS TO EXERCISES

I.   THE WRITING PROCESS

WRITING PROCESS 1d, 1f, and 2c

Answers will vary by student.

WRITING PROCESS 4c

Proofreading
Corrections are highlighted.

Parker ~~p.~~ 1

"Too Much Reality"

Andrea Parker

I have to admit that I am one of the countless Americans sucked into the drama of reality television programs, such as Fox's "Joe Millionaire" and "The Bachelor." But after several years of mindlessly watching other people experience their lives, I'm feeling bored and unchallenged, and even a little insulted. I find myself aimlessly flipping through the channels, longing for a good drama or situation comedy. The problem is, while I've moved on, most network programming hasn't. The reason is simple: networks are raking in big profits from reality television.

II.   WRITING IN COLLEGE AND BEYOND

WRITING ARGUMENTATIVE ESSAYS

4, Distinguishing between Fact and Opinion
(F=Fact; O=Opinion)

1. Higher taxes are not acceptable. (O)

2. A Democrat should win the next presidential election. (O)

3. Some people have a life-threatening allergy to peanuts. (F)

4. Studying history is not relevant to today's workplace. (O)

5. The legal drinking age in most states is twenty-one. (F)

WRITING ARGUMENTATIVE ESSAYS

4a, Facts versus Claims

These are possible answers for claims.

1. (fact) Every American citizen has the right to vote.

   (claim) American citizens have responsibilities.

2. (fact) Some animal rights advocates object to the use of animals for medical research and testing.

   (claim) It is immoral to use animals for medical research and testing.

3. (fact) The obesity rate among children in the U.S. has been steadily growing over the past two decades.

   (claim) American children are not as healthy as they were in the past.

4. (claim) Paintball should be an Olympic medal sport.

   (Fact) Speed skating became a men's Olympic medal sport in 1924.

5. (fact) Thomas Jefferson signed the Declaration of Independence on July 4, 1776.

   (claim) Many men worked to secure American independence during the Revolutionary War.

WRITING ARGUMENTATIVE ESSAYS

4b, Logical Appeals

1. If every family would just recycle its household waste, we wouldn't need to worry about excessive landfills. (Oversimplification)

2. If you vote, then you are a true patriot. (Begging the Question)

3. The governments of Russia and China are similar because they are near each other. (False Analogy)

4. If you really cared about yourself, you would lose weight and lower your blood pressure. (Begging the Question)

5. If the president can afford to send troops around the world, we ought to be able to find a solution to homelessness. (Irrelevant Premises)

ONLINE WRITING

5a, E-mail

1. Subject line is blank; it should instead provide some useful indicator of the message's contents.

2. "Prof." instead of Professor—this is the first of a series of excessively informal choices made by the writer. Note that this is a message from a student to his professor; it should not be overly informal. The same standards generally apply to e-mail at work.

3. "u" instead of "you"; this style is too informal

4. "before" is mispelled

5. "FYI"; this style is too informal

PUBLIC WRITING

7a, Formatting a Business Letter

1. top of page to top of return address: 6–12 line spaces (use this variation to balance the letter visually on the page from top to bottom).

2. line spacing: single-spaced throughout

Check spaces between blocks as they should not all be the same; that is, add space between the date and internal address; internal address and salutation;

155

between the salutation and body text; between the last text block and the close; between the close and signature; and between the signature and notations (if any).

3. Keep paragraphing format style consistent (blocked).

4. Double-space between paragraphs in block style letter.

5. Use accepted postal abbreviations for states (MI).

III.   PARAGRAPHS

PARAGRAPHS

1, Unity

1. <u>Critters other than bears are far more likely to inflict mayhem on your camp.</u> Raccoons, skunks, ring-tailed cats, pack rats, mice, (though often adorable,) and other nighttime invaders are all far more real threats. ~~You will want to dress warm because the temperature can drop dramatically at night.~~ For the most part, the same measures you take against bears will work with other animals. In some established sites, mice can be a real problem. In mouse country try hanging the food bag from the rafter, with a can lid placed halfway down the cord.

   [Source: modified from Kesselheim, Alan. *Canoeing in the Wilderness*. NY: Ragged Mountain Press, 2001. 134-35.]

2. In April General McClellan finally moved his Army of the Potomac against the enemy. ~~The Potomac is a beautiful river.~~ Striking south by way of the peninsula between the James and the York rivers, he prepared to attack Yorktown. The Confederates allowed McClellan to complete his careful, lengthy preparations for the assault, and evacuated the fortress without firing a shot. McClellan then moved in a complicated series of forays. All of McClellan's maneuvers only succeeded in giving President Lincoln~~who was married to Mary Todd Lincoln~~ the idea that he was trying to win the war by tactics rather than by fighting.

   [Source: modified from Jennison, Keith. *The Humorous Mr. Lincoln*. NY: Bonanza Books, n.d. 95.]

PARAGRAPHS

2b, Development Strategies 1

1.   Alan S. Kesselheim's *Canoeing in the Wilderness*:

facts; examples

2.   Keith Jennison's *The Humorous Mr. Lincoln*:

process analysis

PARAGRAPHS

2b, Development Strategies 2 (*THIS SECTION OUT OF PLACE)

Many different strategies could be used, depending on the information students gather, their approach to the material, and their audience. Here are some possibilities:

1. comparison and contrast; facts and statistics

2. examples; facts and statistics; cause and effect

PARAGRAPHS

3, Coherence

1. The narrative follows chronological order: from the time Ponyboy leaves the movie house, is then accosted by the Socs, and finally saved by his fellow Greasers. The narrative is also supported by spatial ordering, as the focus shifts from exiting the movie house to walking home. As Ponyboy walks faster, the scene also intensifies and Ponyboy is jumped by the Socs.

IV.   SENTENCE CLARITY AND STYLE

STYLE

1, Parallelism

Possible rewrites:

1.   I will be making brownies, cookies and a chocolate cake for the bake sale.

2.   When I am in Florida, I enjoy spending time snorkeling, diving, and collecting sea shells.

STYLE

2, Misplaced and Dangling Modifiers

Possible rewrites:

1. John ate the french fries that were dipped in ketchup.

2. The EPA wrote new rules for the spotted owl, which was threatened with extinction.

3. I saw him on the green walkway.

4. Young and inexperienced, Jim discovered that jobs were few and far between.

5. I wrote directions to the house for my friend.

STYLE

3a, Shifts 1

Possible answers.

1. The United Nations' membership has grown steadily, and it adds one or more new members nearly every year. (number shift)

2. The children should keep their lunches and backpacks in their lockers. (person shift)

3. If students wish to order a yearbook, they will want to order early. (number shift)

4. My father worked for forty-two years at General Motors. The corporation made him retire last month. (person shift)

5. If a person wants to fly on a commercial airline, he or she should be aware there is a forty-dollar charge for each carry-on item. (number shift)

STYLE

3b, Shifts 2

Possible answers

1. The students in Ms. Archer's English class wrote essays and performed the play *Romeo and Juliet*.

2. At the surprise party, the cars were parked on another street, the lights were turned off, and the music played softly in the background.

3. Tomorrow we will walk to school but will ride the bus home.

4. The Olympic skaters warmed up before their performances and practiced their most difficult moves.

5. While Harry was on vacation in Ireland, a robber broke into his home.

STYLE

3d, Shifts 3

1. I was screaming as the rollercoaster dropped over sixty feet in 3 seconds. (dangling modifier; subject shift)

2. We all enjoyed the donuts then warmed up by the fire. (voice shift)

3. My new hat wilted as I danced in the pouring rain. (subject shift; dangling modifier)

4. My aunt Charlene swept up the remnants of the broken vase, which was broken into a million pieces. (subject shift; dangling modifier)

5. We saved money by sharing the french fries and ordering the chilidogs, which were buy one get one free. (voice shift)

STYLE

4a, Irrelevant Detail

1. Most spaniels are kept not to be hunters but indoor companions, which is the best place for them.

2. Charles Dickens was a prolific author, working on up to three novels at the same time.

3. Over the last decade the cost of oil has almost doubled, taking up more of Americans' disposable income.

4. Joe proposed to Lisa over our summer vacation.

5. The interstate highway system is now badly in need of extensive rebuilding.

STYLE

4b, Mixed or Illogical Constructions

1. Congressman Jones said that the new spending bill will not increase anyone's taxes.

2. In a bait and switch, a company advertises a product at a very low price to bring in customers, but it does not have enough of that product on hand to meet demand.

3. The baker made a triple chocolate cake; however, he forgot to add baking powder.

4. We were skiing down the north side of the mountain when we crashed into a clump of evergreens.

5. Can you lend me the new Stephen King book you just finished reading?

STYLE

5a, Subordination—Choppy Sentences

Possible rewrites:

1. Add the flour after the yeast and liquids rise in the bowl, and then knead the dough, adding flour until it no longer sticks to your fingers.

2. The quote for the new family room is out of our price range, so we will put off adding the new addition until next year.

3. I do my research at our university library because its one million plus volumes provide coverage that is both in-depth and up-to-date.

4. I am trying to lose weight by eating salads every day, but I am not sure if I can lose two dress sizes by our summer vacation.

5. The Statue of Liberty, a gift from the French people and dedicated in 1886, was restored for its centennial and once again looks beautiful.

STYLE

5c, Coordination—Ideas of Equal Importance

Possible rewrites:

1. Because I had not eaten for seven hours, I ate an entire pizza when I finally got home.

2. While I believe he is guilty of stealing the other students' lunches, there are extenuating circumstances.

3. My great-uncle neither smokes nor drinks.

4. Joe is not only a star athlete on the baseball and football teams, but he also plays the violin in the orchestra.

5. This rain is good for people; it is filling the reservoirs.

STYLE

6b, Logical Order

Possible rewrites:

1. Glen Close arrived in a silver gown by Oscar de la Renta, won an Oscar, and danced at an exclusive party until six in the morning.

2. Bonds had a terrible day when we were at the ballpark; he struck out in the first, fifth, and seventh innings.

3. I like a movie if it begins well, has a good story, and ends happily.

4. Kelly delivered her baby after six hours of labor, and we counted the baby's toes.

5. As I examined the antique, I saw the paint had been restored and the back had several deep scratches.

STYLE

6c, Active Voice

Possible rewrites:

1. Grandma bought the decorations, balloons, food, and cake.

2. The plastic surgeon stitched the deep gash on Don's face.

3. The county sheriff gave the teenager a speeding ticket.

4. The wind pushed the kite into the power lines.

5. My boss gave me an ultimatum as soon as I returned from Phoenix.

STYLE

7a, Sentence Variety 1

Possible rewrites:

1. The farm workers labored in the fields all day and quickly ate all the sandwiches and salad we gave them.

2. While Don and Susan are a nice, young couple, they are too young to get married.

3. Because Hurricane Katrina devastated New Orleans and most of the Gulf Coast, people from around the country worked together to ease the suffering of those who were affected.

4. As you fly over any major U.S. city, look out the plane's window; you will be shocked by the number of swimming pools you will see.

5. While many students fail accounting because it is a difficult class, John got an "A."

STYLE

7b, Sentence Variety 2

Possible rewrites:

1. To be ready to plant outside in the spring, I planted the dahlia bulbs indoors in January and watered them every day.

2. Planting the dahlia bulbs indoors in January, I watered them every day so they would be ready to plant outside in the spring.

3. Because I wanted the dahlias to be ready to plant outside in the spring, I planted the dahlia bulbs indoors in January and watered them every day.

4. In January, I planted the dahlia bulbs indoors and watered them every day, so they would be ready to plant outside in the spring.

5. To crush those who did not support the revolution, French revolutionaries began *The Reign of Terror* in 1789.

V. WORD CHOICE

WORDS

1, Eliminating Clutter

Possible answers:

1. The famous actor asked for a seat in the back of the restaurant so he would not be bothered by his fans.

2. Kelly was the only person alone in the office Wednesday night, so she must be the one who stole the money from the cash box.

3. The children were told that sending text messages during dinner was rude.

4. The musicians could not even play the national anthem without mistakes.

5. Why do schools of swimming fish and flocks of flying birds move with a similar coordinated motion?

WORDS

2c, General versus Specific Words

Possible answers:

1. books: mystery; romance; science fiction

2. animals: leopards; squirrels; dogs

3. ice cream: rocky road; chocolate; moose tracks

4. governments: democracy; republic

5. holidays: New Year's Day; Valentine's Day

WORDS

2c, Abstract versus Concrete Words

1. brilliant: abstract

2. trophy: concrete

3. test: concrete

4. purple: abstract

5. stars: concrete

WORDS

2d, Idioms

1. The mother rewarded the boy with a chocolate ice cream cone.

2. Kelly arrived early at the bookstore so that she would be sure to get an autograph.

3. Please use the tool for the purpose it was intended.

4. Brick is superior to wood when building a house in this part of the country.

5. I want to improve my jump shot for the next game.

WORDS

3a–b, Appropriate Formality

Possible answers:

1. There are so many preparations to make before the wedding.

2. The new Danielle Steele book is compelling and well written.

3. You will need to drive faster if you want to arrive at the theater before the movie starts.

4. Collecting stamps was Phil's hobby.

5. Janet was disappointed that Paul did not call her back for a second date.

WORDS

4, Bias in Writing

Possible answers:

1. Police officers should always remember to wear their badges.

2. I will tip twenty percent to servers who provide excellent service.

3. Each congressional senator voted in favor of the bill.

4. Mail carriers who work in California should wear a strong sunscreen every day.

5. Of all creatures on the planet, people are the most intelligent and the most destructive.

WORDS

5, The Dictionary

1. There are three syllables in "as•tro•naut," and there are four in "e•mo•tion•al."

2. magazine: a periodic publication. Developed from the more general word "store house."

3. manner: from the Latin "manus," or hand; practice or execution of the arts.

4. poet: from the Greek "poiein," meaning to create.

5. There are three syllables in porcupine "por•cu•pine."

WORDS

6, The Thesaurus direct

1. **document** (noun): formal piece of writing; manuscript; computer file; (verb): to record information; to support with evidence; (antonym): (adjective): undocumented

2. **translate** (verb): turn words into different language; to change form; to decipher; to interpret; to explain (antonym): (adjective): inexplicable

Copyright © 2011, 2008, 2005, Pearson Education, Inc.

3. **end** (noun): extremity of object; final part; termination (verb): to stop; to finish (antonym): (noun): beginning

4. **foul** (noun): an illegal action in sports;(adjective): disgusting; contaminated; dirty; inclement (antonym): (adjective) clean

5. **limit** (noun): farthest point; maximum allowed; boundary (verb): control; reduce (antonym): (adjective): limitless

VI. SENTENCE PARTS AND PATTERNS

SENTENCES

1a, Verbs

1. We <u>climbed</u> <u>the mountain</u> and reached the summit before sundown.

     VT   DO

2. My sister Jane <u>gave</u> <u>our parents</u> <u>a fiftieth anniversary party</u>.

            VT IO   DO

3. The weather <u>seems</u> <u>fine</u> today.

            VL   PA

4. We <u>picked up</u> <u>a sandwich</u> for lunch at the diner on the corner.

     VT   DO

5. The sandwiches <u>were</u> <u>delicious</u>.

           VL PA

166

SENTENCES

1a, Nouns

	singular	plural	sing. possessive	pl. possessive
1.	lamp	lamps	lamp's	lamps'
2.	apple	apples	apple's	apples'
3.	suitcase	suitcases	suitcase's	suitcases'
4.	doctor	doctors	doctor's	doctors'
5.	shark	sharks	shark's	sharks'

SENTENCES

1a, Pronouns

1. Can <u>you</u> tell where <u>I</u> had the plastic surgery?

2. <u>I</u> fell asleep while Mr. White was giving <u>his</u> speech.

3. Carla usually has <u>her</u> hair styled before a big date.

4. The child had chocolate ice cream melting down <u>his</u> chin.

5. Can <u>you</u> tell <u>me</u> how to get to the apple orchard?

SENTENCES

1a, Adjectives

1. The Millennium Force is Cedar Point's (tall, taller, <u>tallest</u>) roller coaster.

2. The waves at Tanner Beach are (big, <u>bigger</u>, biggest) than those at West Beach and East Beach.

3. July 22, 1922 was the (hot, hotter, <u>hottest</u>) day ever recorded in Detroit, Michigan.

4. I cannot decide which is (delicious, <u>more delicious</u>, the most delicious)—the cannoli or the chocolate cream pie.

5. Before starting the race, the judge called, "May the (good, better, <u>best</u>) cyclist win!"

SENTENCES

1a, Adverbs

1. The <u>finely</u> chopped onions sizzled <u>slowly</u> in the frying pan.

2. Please sit <u>quietly</u>.

3. We were happy to learn that Grandmother would arrive <u>very</u> <u>shortly</u>.

4. After the thunderstorm, steam rose <u>eerily</u> from the <u>still</u>-warm pavement.

5. The builders worked <u>carefully</u> and <u>diligently</u> to finish the biggest project of the year.

SENTENCES

1a, Prepositions

1. Please leave the sauce simmering (<u>on</u> the stove) (<u>for</u> thirty minutes).

2. Most dolphins have acute eyesight (<u>in</u> the water).

3. All the Muscat grapes (<u>in</u> the orchard) were destroyed (<u>by</u> frost).

4. We rode our bikes (<u>down</u> the steep hill) and (<u>into</u> the next town).

5. Forty-seven stories (<u>above</u> the street), the birds built their nest (<u>on</u> one) (<u>of</u> the Chrysler Building's ledges).

SENTENCES

1a, Conjunctions

1. We paid for the popcorn (and we went back to our seats). (COORD)

2. The earthquake shook the small village, (but none of the villagers were injured). (COORD).

3. (Although the lawyer was a Harvard Law School graduate), his fees were quite reasonable. (SUB)

4. (Neither Kevin nor Sam) wants to travel to the coast this weekend. (CORREL)

5. (Unless you sign the release form), your child will not be able to attend summer camp. (SUB)

SENTENCES

1b, Subjects

1. <u>Billy's sense of humor</u> kept the crowd laughing all night.

2. <u>The neighbor's black and white pit bull, named Sly</u>, always greets us with a wagging tail.

3. <u>Mrs. Smith's fruit pies</u> are on sale this week.

4. When the <u>Canadian skiers</u> reached the top of the mountain, they plotted their course down.

5. The last time that I checked, <u>the university</u> had five libraries.

SENTENCES

1b, Predicates

1. Smoking <u>is expensive and addictive.</u>

2. Jerry <u>wanted to attend medical school on the East Coast.</u>

3. The manager <u>was skilled at calming angry customers.</u>

4. The soldiers <u>received their orders and prepared for life in Afghanistan.</u>

5. After working together all day, Bill and Ted <u>cooked dinner together also.</u>

SENTENCES

1b. Objects

1. Tamara threw <u>the flowers</u> <u>in Jack's face</u>. (DO, IO)
2. My boss loves <u>money</u>. (DO)
3. The bank robbers terrorized <u>the customers</u> and stole <u>the money</u>. (DO, DO)
4. The mother hid <u>the chips and cookies</u> in the back cupboard. (DO)
5. Julia asked <u>me</u> to take her to the mall. (DO)

169

SENTENCES

1c Prepositional Phrases

1. The girl hid (under the bed) (until her mother came home).

2. To get (to the grocery store), (go over the next hill) (to the end) (of the street) and turn left.

3. The hot sauce (on the table) will make you cry.

4. The car (with the dent) (on the front fender) is my sister's.

5. The temperature (in the hockey stadium) is dropping fast.

SENTENCES

1c, Verbals

1. The girl <u>selling</u> cookies door-to-door plans to stay on her side of town. (PRES PART)

2. <u>Pacing yourself</u> during an exam is crucial. (GER)

3. The man <u>plowing the street</u> is not wearing a hat or gloves. (PRES PART)

4. The Continental Army, <u>faced with many hardships</u>, managed <u>to defeat</u> the <u>better trained and equipped British</u>. (PAST PART; INF; PAST PART)

5. <u>To request more funding,</u> you will need <u>to speak with the president</u> of the company. (INF; INF)

SENTENCES

1d, Clauses

1. The tennis player, <u>who injured his knee during the last match,</u> is forfeiting. (ADJ CLS)

2. I realized Joe was an ungrateful boyfriend <u>who would be eating alone tonight.</u> (ADJ CLS)

3. The antique was damaged <u>after we moved.</u> (ADV CLS)

4. <u>Before I leave for France,</u> I want to contact the post office to stop my mail. (ADV CLS)

5. After losing three games straight, the team was ecstatic <u>when it beat the undefeated first place team.</u> (ADV CLS)

SENTENCES

1e, Types of Sentences

1. Though I exercise every day, I still cannot lose those final ten pounds. (complex)

2. Bill runs in Central Park. (simple)

3. Joe will travel to Africa this summer, and his children will stay with their grandparents in Rhode Island. (compound)

4. After scooping ice cream all summer, my right arm was so strong that I could beat my older brother in arm wrestling, and my left arm looked so withered to me that it seemed almost like the forelegs of *Tyrannosaurus rex*. (compound-complex)

5. The alligator stared at us from the swampy waters, but we felt safe on the boat. (compound)

SENTENCES

2, Subject-Verb Agreement 1

1. The ticket, including dinner with dessert, a floor show, and dancing after, costs only twenty dollars.

2. There are usually some teachers who are willing to chaperone the prom.

3. Neither the potato salad nor the fruit salad was very cold.

4. The Civil War exhibit and The Revolutionary War documentary offer a glimpse into the past.

5. High tides and wind create dangerous conditions along the coast.

SENTENCES

2 e–I, Subject-Verb Agreement 2

1. Anything you donate goes to a good cause.

2. Dave is the only one at the party who always leaves early.

3. None of my classes meets before 10 a.m.

4. There are, though our firm tries to hide it, financial difficulties.

5. Politics both fascinates and repulses him.

SENTENCES

3a–b, Principal Parts of Irregular Verbs

1. If you bend the pipe more, I think it will fit.

2. The squirrels dug in the garden looking for radishes.

3. The senator spoke last week at the Democratic fundraiser.

4. The patient had been struck with the swine flu before his surgery.

5. I saw that new movie with Robert Pattinson last week.

SENTENCES

3c, Verb Tense

1. PRESENT PERFECT: The sun has risen over the horizon every morning.

2. PRESENT PROGRESSIVE: The sun is going to rise over the horizon every morning.

3. PRESENT PERFECT PROGRESSIVE: The sun has been rising over the horizon every morning.

4. PAST: The sun rose over the horizon every morning.

5. PAST PERFECT: The sun had risen over the horizon every morning.

SENTENCES

3e, Verb Mood

1. (subjunctive) Bob asked that Joe come early today.

2. (imperative) Clean your room and take out the trash.

3. (indicative) Every night he reads until bedtime.

4. (imperative) Mary said, "Hurry up, or we'll miss the bus."

5. (subjunctive) I wished I would win the lottery, but I was unlucky.

SENTENCES

3f, Active and Passive Voices

1. (active) The executive committee wrote a report.

172

2. (passive) Chess was played by the students in Ms. Biddle's class.

3. (passive) The book titled *Twilight* was loved by the girls in the bookstore.

4. (passive) The Blue Line bus was seen by Regina.

5. (active) Many people who rarely watch baseball otherwise watch the World Series.

SENTENCES

4a, Pronoun Agreement

1. The jury provided its decision to the judge.

2. Every morning Buster frightens the mail carrier, Joe, who is afraid of dogs.

3. Neither the cook nor the server pays for his own meal.

4. When Louisa and Hal come to visit, they always bring their dog.

5. Each man worked on his soccer skills.

SENTENCES

4b Pronoun Reference

1. The recent drought could be a problem. Note: Students may insert other ideas for the word *that*.

2. My husband, whose garden grows beautiful vegetables, eats them every day.

3. Though I know that supply-side economics focuses on production, and demand-side economics emphasizes consumption, this knowledge has never helped me understand where my paycheck goes every week.

4. If my medical insurance company denies the claim, it will be speaking to my attorney.

5. When tours come through our town, they often stop at the Shelburne Museum to see its extensive American folk art collection.

SENTENCES

4c, Pronoun Case 1

1. Have you seen my brother?

2. My sister and I went to the new shopping center.

3. According to Julia and me, Pizza Pit has the best pizza in town.

4. The boss appreciated their working on Saturday night.

5. My sister said she would be going to visit our grandmother after visiting Susan and me.

SENTENCES

4c–d, Pronoun Case 2

1. The attorney asked my mother and me to sit down before he read the will.

2. Despite all his campaigning, the incumbent was running stronger than he, as the *New York Times* reported.

3. The teacher called Denny, Mindy and me to the front of the classroom.

4. My sister, who has incredibly acute hearing when it comes to the telephone, yelled out from the shower, "Whom is that call for?"

5. Free pine tree saplings will be given to whoever asks.

SENTENCES

5, Adjectives and Adverbs

1. The caterer felt bad that the food was cold and undercooked.

2. That green blouse looks good with your black jacket.

3. Stretch your legs well before you start the race.

4. The professor looked curiously at their group project.

5. With two of their starters on the disabled list, things look bad for the Seattle Mariners.

SENTENCES

6, Sentence Fragments 1

Possible rewrites:

1. F: Despite the hours of work he committed to the project, he did not get a raise.

2. S:

3. F: As long as you support your point, you can write a good argument.

4. S

5. F, S: The cat that climbed the tree is a stray.

SENTENCES

6, Sentence Fragments 2

Possible rewrites:

1. The boy loves his great aunt and visits her every day.

2. My big brother Todd likes to dance, especially to hip-hop music.

3. The menu highlighted my two favorite meals, shrimp scampi and seafood Alfredo.

4. My brother and his wife and my husband and I bought tickets to the Billy Joel concert.

5. When I saw the *Mona Lisa* in person, I was, to be honest, disappointed.

SENTENCES

7, Comma Splices 1

Possible rewrites:

1. The price of plane tickets is rising, so I hope I saved enough money.

2. Professor Gerson has a pleasantly acid sense of humor; accordingly, he quipped that the term *European ally* is an oxymoron.

3. The music is too loud. Turn it down.

4. The man was arrested as he arrived home and he was charged with armed robbery.

5. The backpackers were prepared for any type of weather, and they were glad to have brought their rain gear.

7, Comma Splices 2

Possible rewrites:

1. We studied about the witch hunt in Europe, but the class had many misconceptions about witches.

175

2. With all the channel choices on cable and satellite TV these days, I wish there were something good to watch. It seems like there were better programs when I had fewer choices.

3. Only take one dessert. We have a large crowd tonight.

4. They weren't important ideas; however, they were interesting suggestions.

5. I'm not sure if we should purchase the house now because I think housing prices will fall next month.

SENTENCES

7, Run-on Sentences 1

Possible rewrites:

1. The large trout jerked on the hook fiercely. It broke the line and swam away.

2. Although I love spaghetti and meatballs, I rarely eat in Italian restaurants.

3. Because I have been indoors all week, I feel like lying in the sun.

4. I know what an armadillo looks like, but I'm not quite sure what an aardvark looks like.

5. The last U.S. space shuttle flight to *Mir* was made in 1999; since then, all shuttle flights have been to the new International Space Station.

SENTENCES

7, Run-on Sentences 2

Possible answers:

1. We packed apples and peanut butter and jelly sandwiches.

2. The veal parmesan and the dessert were excellent.

3. Janel got an A on her essay, so she must have written many drafts.

4. The preschoolers boarded the bus after the zoo tour and the parents fell asleep on the way home.

5. During the snowstorm, the city workers plowed the streets and the citizens shoveled the sidewalks.

VII.   PUNCTUATION

PUNCTUATION

1a–c, The Comma 1

1. As I felt the warm water hit my skin, I closed my eyes and took a deep breath.

2. I have known Bob all my life, yet I am not sure where he works.

3. Laughing, the teenagers piled into a small booth.

4. The best dessert on the menu, the tiramisu, is sold out tonight.

5. My oldest brother, Geoffrey, usually comes for Thanksgiving.

PUNCTUATION

1d–g, The Comma 2

1. The car was described as having tinted windows, a sunroof, and a ed pinstripe.

2. This fall Eliot was reading Ernest Hemingway, Maya Angelou, and Alice Walker.

3. Because they did not honor the contract, we will not do business with them again.

4. President Jimmy Carter may turn out to be more effective out of office than in, unlike Lyndon Johnson.

5. Eating plenty of fiber will help you feel full, lose weight, and improve digestion.

PUNCTUATION

1h–l, The Comma 3

1. I smiled and said, "Yes, I'll be there."

2. If you want to call, Jessica has a phone.

3. Our spring break runs from Monday, March 15, through Monday, March 22.

4. My sister called yesterday and asked, "Guess who is having a baby?"

5. Lonnie gave me a ride from Tulsa, Oklahoma, to Paris, Texas.

PUNCTUATION

1m, The Comma 4

1. The two water spaniels and their owner swam across the pond and dried off in the hot sun.

2. To my Aunt Mary, my youngest brother could do no wrong.

3. Larry and Anna Marie did not like dogs until they met Buster.

4. You should probably use a strong sunscreen before you go to the beach.

5. The small gold locket was a family heirloom.

PUNCTUATION

2, The Semicolon

1. I waited in line for four hours to get the tickets, but I didn't mind, nor did my sister.

2. The rapid decrease in computer hardware prices has put pressure on software developers to do the same; nonetheless, they have resisted the trend for the most part.

3. On one recent weekend I saw *Pearl Harbor*, which used extensive computer-generated simulations of an historical event; *The Matrix*, which explored virtual worlds accessed via mind control; and *Until the End of the World*, which presented computer-driven dream exploration.

4. I planted the sickly looking plant in the spring; it blossomed into a beautiful flowering shrub by summer.

5. Because there are so many errors when I use my GPS, I prefer a hand-written map.

PUNCTUATION

3, The Colon

1. Remember our mission statement: "We help students develop the skills to become independent, self-sufficient adults who contribute to society."

2. Scientists, in an effort to isolate what it is in food that makes most people evaluate it as "tasting good or delicious," have determined the single most important ingredient: fat.

3. When you go to the grocery store please purchase bread, butter, eggs, and chocolate milk.

4. The conditions are perfect for planting flowers: rich soil, plenty of sunshine, and a forecast for rain.

5. We took the following route: Route 80 to Rock Springs, Route 187 to Farson, and Route 28 to South Pass City.

PUNCTUATION

4, The Apostrophe

1. We have forty dogs at the dog kennel, and we trim every dog's fur for the summer weather.

2. My grandmother told me that the '38 hurricane was much worse than this year's storm.

3. We watched the bird make its nest from the dryer lint.

4. The comedian's humor fell flat with the late night crowd.

5. I thought it was hers, but perhaps it's really Bill's.

PUNCTUATION

5, Quotation Marks

1. "Where you place your commas is one of my teacher's pet peeves, so I always double check my work," said Elaine.

2. "Where would you like us to place the new furniture?" asked the movers.

3. My two favorite poems are "The Mending Wall" by Robert Frost and "A Shady Friend" by Emily Dickinson.

4. Do not confuse the word "implicit" with the word "explicit."

5. "Do you think the train ride to Chicago will be boring?" asked Carl.

   "No," I replied, "I will bring crossword puzzles, books and some snacks."

   "What can I bring?" asked Carl.

PUNCTUATION

6a, The Period

1. Dr. Craig is one of the most respected plastic surgeons in Michigan.

2. FEMA is an agency of the United States Department of Homeland Security.

3. I wondered if he knew what the USDA stamp on the meat stood for.

4. When addressing a letter, the state of Florida is abbreviated as FL.

5. Tintin's best friend is Capt. Horatio Haddock.

PUNCTUATION

6b–c, The Question Mark and Exclamation Point

1. The bus driver asked, "Is there anyone on the bus who lives at the end of Cole Street?"

2. John exclaimed, "I have the winning ticket!"

3. Which route to Des Moines has less traffic, John wanted to know.

4. "Why do you always throw your coffee grounds in the garden?"

5. My boss asked me whether I wanted to be on the blue team or the green team.

PUNCTUATION

6d–h, Other Punctuation

Possible Rewrites:

1. Barack Obama, the current president of the United States, is our forty-fourth president.

2. When in Rome—as the saying goes—do as the Romans do.

3. Maya Angelou's beautiful words hit home: "a bird doesn't sing because it has an answer / it sings because it has a song."

4. "Our class meets in that new science building. What's its name? Something Hall ... Burstein ... Gurstein? I can't remember," said John.

5. I still remember the opening lines to Shakespeare's Sonnet LXXIII: "That time of year thou mayst in me behold / When yellow leaves, or none, or few, do hang / Upon those boughs which shake against the cold."

VIII. MECHANICS

MECHANICS

1a–d, Capitals 1

1. People who live in the south are more comfortable with hot weather.

2. When James "Joe" Jackson sang last week at the Hartford Avenue Grill, the crowd roared its approval.

3. The sky was so clear last night that we could see the North Star.

4. The women's conference will feature several famous African American authors.

5. In the last four months, the Missouri and Mississippi rivers reached record flood levels, but the Hudson River was below normal.

MECHANICS

1e–j, Capitals 2

1. In a recent article, commentator Julia Webb wrote, "For the first time in U.S. history, by the year 2002, more than fifty percent of all American jobs will require at least one year of college."

2. Did you read Mitch Albom's article today's *Detroit News*?

3. My favorite courses this term are English, calculus and history.

4. I think she bought one of the new Apple notebook computers.

5. The news media program I watch the most is *The O'Reilly Factor* on Fox News Channel.

MECHANICS

2, Abbreviations

1. Our history teacher asked us to read chapter 18 before class tomorrow.

2. The new department chair will be here next week. She is from New York City.

3. Aristotle was born in 384 B.C.

4. According to the town historian, the house was built circa 1900.

5. You will need to order four dozen company shirts for the team conference.

10. British and American English differ in many small ways; for example, we place a period after the abbreviation for *Mister* (Mr.), whereas the British do not.

MECHANICS

3, Numbers

1. The price of milk this week is $3.09.

2. Charles Lindbergh began his historic two-day flight on May 20, 1927, from Roosevelt Field, Long Island.

3. Renting a bike on the island can more than $20 [or twenty dollars] an hour.

4. The local factory employs over 300 people.

5. Over the holidays we saw four films, two plays, and thirteen videos. [or 4 films, 2 plays, and 13 videos]

MECHANICS

4, Italics/Underlining

1. Linda likes Microsoft *Word*, but I prefer *WordPerfect*.

2. It is important to seek marriage counseling *before* you get married.

3. I asked him to explain what *noblesse oblige* means.

4. I read about all the flooding in the south in *The Detroit News*.

5. Tina objected to Dickens's frequent use of a *deus ex machina* to resolve his fantastically-plotted novels.

MECHANICS

5, The Hyphen

1. To avoid my ex-husband, I never drive down Fifth Street.

2. The ex-Metropolitan Opera soprano joined our community chorus and improved the entire section's performance.

3. The administration struggles to find new teachers before the start of the school year.

4. He was elected President of The Library Board by a vote of twenty-one to sixteen.

5. In pre-revolutionary America, the colonists were subjects of the king of England.

MECHANICS

6a, Basic Spelling Rules

1. Ask the neighbors if they would like to come over for grilled burgers and hot dogs.

2. Professor Guimard is very knowledgeable about plate tectonics.

3. Lorraine was lying down thinking when an idea suddenly occurred to her; half an hour later she had laid out all the fundamentals in the field of astronomy.

4. Use your best judgment when selecting the vegetable plants.

5. You should receive the check in the mail early next week.

MECHANICS

6b, Words that Sound Alike

1. As I walked up the mountain, I found myself gasping for breath.

2. In the 100-meter finals, Sarah was third and I was fourth.

3. Please choose a game piece.

4. My teacher recommended that we always read the foreword, as it usually defines the scope and approach of the book that follows.

5. I prefer coarse ground pepper on my salad.

IX. RESEARCH WRITING

Research exercises are incorporated into chapter XI, MLA Style, Documentation, and Format; chapter XII, APA Style, Documentation, and Format; and chapter XIII, CMS and CSE-Style, Documentation and Format.

X. WRITING IN THE DISCIPLINES

DISCIPLINES

1a, Understand Your Writing Assignment

Answers will vary by student.

DISCIPLINES

1b, e Methods/Evidence and Documentation/Format

1. Primary sources are original documents written or captured by those who experienced and witnessed events firsthand. Examples will vary by student.

2. Secondary sources are documents one or more steps removed from the events or objects which are their subjects. Examples will vary by student.

DISCIPLINES

2d, Conventions for Writing about Literature

Answers vary by student.

DISCIPLINES

2d, 3d, 4d, and 5d Conventions

All Disciplines

    1. first, second

Literature

    2. summarizing

    3. full name; last name

    4. present; past

XI. MLA-STYLE, DOCUMENTATION, AND FORMAT

MLA

Questions

    1. Modern Language Association

184

2. in-text citations and works cited page

3. They immediately let readers know the source of a citation without breaking the flow of the paper.

4. author's last name and page number

5. Two or three authors must include all authors' names within the signal phrase or in the parentheses; for works with more than three authors, include only the last name of the first author, followed by the Latin phrase *et al.*

MLA

2, Avoiding Plagiarism

Because there are infinitely many possible correct paraphrases of the quotations provided, it is left to the instructor to review and assess each student's work for this exercise.

MLA

3, Integrating Borrowed Material.

Because there are infinitely many possible correct ways to incorporate these quotations, it is left to the instructor to review and assess each student's work for this exercise.

MLA

1a, In-Text Citations

Note: Possible answers are provided, but many other valid solutions exist.

1. The story begins in the middle of the action: "At last there were footsteps, several sets of heavy boots clomping in the corridor. A key turned in the lock. I sat up in bed and cracked my skull against the ceiling, hard enough that I bit through my lip" (Benioff 39).

2. David Benioff begins his novel *City of Thieves* in the middle of the action: "At last there were footsteps, several sets of heavy boots clomping in the corridor. A key turned in the lock. I sat up in bed and cracked my skull against the ceiling, hard enough that I bit through my lip" (39).

3. The democrats are applauding the president for his proposal "to link federal dollars to initiatives like ending the achievement gap between white and non-white students, evaluating teachers and awarding performance bonuses to principals and teachers who earn them" (Bloomberg and Klein 49).

4. According to Bloomberg and Klein's article in *Time,* "Making the Grade," the Democrats are applauding the president for his proposal "to link federal

185

dollars to initiatives like ending the achievement gap between white and non-white students, evaluating teachers and awarding performance bonuses to principals and teachers who earn them" (49).

5. Bill Streever points out in his book *Cold* that "at thirty two degrees, the water starts to freeze…Newly frozen water is nine percent bigger than liquid water" (34–35).

MLA

5, Manuscript Format

(a) <u>top of page</u> to <u>last name/page number</u>: 1/2 inch

1. (b) top and bottom margins: 1 inch

2 (c) line spacing: double-spaced

3. (d) left margin: 1 inch

4. (e) right margin: 1 inch

5. (f) "Smith page 3" should instead be "Smith 3"—"page" shouldn't be written out.

MLA

1c, Formatting a Works Cited Page

Works Cited

"Attention-Deficit Hyperactivity Disorder." *National Institute of Mental*

Health. 25 March 2010

<http://www.nimh.nih.gov/health/publiations/attention-deficit-

hyperactivity-disorder>.

Epstein, Jeffery, et al. "Attention-Deficit Hyperactivity Disorder

Outcomes for Children Treated in Community-Based Pediatric

Settings." *Archives of Pediatrics & Adolescent Medicine* 164.2 (2010):

11+. <u>Expanded Academic Index.</u> Info Trac. 25 March 2010.

186

XII. APA-STYLE, DOCUMENTATION, AND FORMAT

APA

Questions

1. American Psychological Association

2. brief in-text citation and reference page

3. They immediately let readers know the source of a citation without breaking the flow of the paper.

4. author's last name, year of publication

5. For two authors, list both authors' names in the text with year of publication immediately following, or put both names in a parenthetical citation, using an ampersand between the names. For three to five authors, give all authors' last names in the text or parentheses in your first citation only. Use an ampersand instead of *and* in the parenthetical citation. In subsequent citations, use only the first author's name and *et al.* For a work with six or more authors, in all citations, use the first author's name, followed by *et al.*

APA

5, Manuscript format

    (a)   <u>top of page</u> to <u>Title/page number</u>: 1/2 inch

1.   (b) top and bottom margins: 1 inch

2.   (c) line spacing: double-spaced

3.   (d) left margin: 1 inch

4.   (e) right margin: 1 inch

5.   (f) "Smith page 3" should instead be "Rise and Fall 3"—the student's name is not included, nor is the word "page," and the page number should be preceded by a shortened version of the paper's title (here given as "Rise and Fall").

Reference Page

References

Carlton, J. (2009). Solar panels generate energy and arguments. *The Wall Street*

 Journal Online. Retrieved from

 http://www.realestatejournal.com/homegarden/20040608-carlton.html

Foster, K., Hindman, D., & Stelmack, A. (2007). *Sustainable residential*

 interiors. Hoboken: John Wiley & Sons, Inc.

Kennedy, J.L. (2009). Alternative energy, climate change proposals.

 Pennsylvania Law Weekly 3(12), 79–84.

CMS DOCUMENTATION AND FORMAT
CSE-STYLE DOCUMENTATION

CMS

Questions

1. *The Chicago Manual of Style*

2. series of raised Arabic numerals placed after each item being acknowledged that refer to endnotes at the end of the paper; and a bibliography that provides complete data for sources cited in the paper, as well as some consulted but not actually cited

3. They let readers know that a source is used.

4. Elements include complete publication data, including the page number for the material you are quoting, paraphrasing, or summarizing.

5. Use normal order for all names after the first, using commas to separate the names with an *and* before the last author's name.

CMS

CMS Bibliography

Bibliography

Anbinder, Tyler. "Which Poor Man's Fight? Immigrants and the Federal Conscription of 1863," *Civil War History*, December 2006, http://80-find.galegroup.com/.

Craughwell, Thomas. "Stealing Lincoln's Body." *Journal of the Abraham Lincoln Association* 29.1 (Winter 2008): 79–87. http://historycooperative.org/jornals/jala/29.1/index.html (accessed March 25, 2010).

Jennison, Keith. *The Humorous Mr. Lincoln.* New York: Bantam Books, 1965.

Marvel, William, "Staying the Course at Gettysburg," *Civil War Times*, April 2010, 40.

Peters, Arthur. *Seven Trails West.* New York: Abbeville Press, 1996.

Rothstein, Edward. "Reconsidering the Man From Illinois." *New York Times*, December 11, 2008, Arts section, Midwest edition.

CSE

Questions

1. names. For three or more authors, use the first author's last name followed by *et al.*

2. References or Cited References

3. List references in the order in which they are cited in the paper and number them accordingly.

CSE

CSE References Page

Cited References

1. Hentz PS. Rescuing wildlife: A guide to helping injured and orphaned animals. Mechanicsburg (PA): Stackpole Books: 2009. 130 p.

2. Jones T. 2008 IUCN red list of threatened species [serial on the Internet]. 2008 [cited 2010 mar 25]; available from: http://www.iucnredlist.org

XIV. ESL BASICS

A Note to Instructors: The exercise book includes the following message for students:

AN IMPORTANT REMINDER FOR STUDENTS: Because of the flexibility of the English language, there may be more than one way to correct the errors in each exercise. This is particularly true in this chapter. If you have any questions about your answers versus the ones supplied in the Selected Answers section, please ask your instructor. Very likely there will be other students with the same or similar questions.

Instructors are, therefore, encouraged to solicit a variety of answers from their students and to discuss them with the class, thereby making public teaching points of what might otherwise remain private confusions.

ESL

1a, Modals

1. By the end of the day, John will be done weeding the garden.

2. Next season's team will play soccer on the football field.

3. Do you think you will visit us this summer in Florida?

4. Because Lily is grounded, she cannot play with us in the park.

5. When I was growing up, my family usually would take a trip in the summer.

ESL

1b, Perfect Tenses

1. My aunts have made over three thousand pieces of bead jewelry.

2. The football players have been eating all day.

3. Bill goes to the movies frequently; he will have seen the latest comedy already.

4. Chloë had sung in the choir for three years before she was chosen to be its director.

5. Suzanne has flown into Detroit over three times in the last year.

ESL

1c, Progressive Tenses

1. John is seeing Reno for the first time.

2. The college is giving away free textbooks.

3. The ozone layer has been thinning because of the release of harmful chemicals.

4. My boss is unhappy because I arrived late to work today and missed the meeting.

5. Sanga had been thinking calculus was easy until he took the midterm exam.

ESL

1d, Passive Voice 1

1. The NBA championship was won by San Antonio this year.

2. The national anthem is played before every hockey game.

3. We could not believe we were seated next to the president of the United States.

4. Many instructions are now written in both English and Spanish.

5. Every student is expected to do well in his or her studies.

ESL

1d, Passive Voice 2

1. Terusuke lost my backpack yesterday.

2. Many young women wear lip gloss.

3. Bizet wrote *Carmen*.

4. The new tax on cigarettes angers many citizens.

5. The library staff saved the books.

1e, Two-Word Verbs

1. Where's the newspaper? Oh, John threw it away.

2. The police officer helped out the motorist after the accident.

3. Because of the extensive fire damage, the fire marshal ordered the building's owners to tear it down.

4. The survivors clung to the boat.

5. Why doesn't he pick on someone his own size?

1f, Verbals

1. They agreed to come over here before the game.

2. Josef misses eating home-cooked meals.

3. My personal trainer helped me take off ten pounds in two weeks.

4. My brother thinks acting is an exciting profession.

5. When I finish eating, I'll read to you.

2a–c, Count and Noncount Nouns 1

1. Gordon knows a lot of local history.

2. How many loaves of bread do you need for your dinner party?

3. Please empty the sand out of your shoes before you get into the car.

4. Guadalupe said many machines are built there.

5. How many pieces of fish do you think the boys will eat?

2a–c, Count and Noncount Nouns 2

1. Gianni lost his cash through a hole in his pocket.

2. Do you have enough quarters for the vending machine?

3. How many people will be at the wedding shower?

4. Is Karen still looking for a place to live?

5. You have my full confidence.

ESL

2c–d, Articles

1. An hour ago he left for the office.

2. The first assignment is to read chapter one of the classroom textbook.

3. When she finishes high school, she wants to travel before finding employment.

4. It is a short trip to the coast.

5. George tried many odd jobs before joining the Navy.

ESL

2d, Definite Article

1. Please pass the ketchup.

2. Highway 62 is the easiest way to get to the amusement park.

3. We saw the young man who was elected Mayor of Hamburg.

4. Hockey is very popular here.

5. I saw Bob walking down the hall just a minute ago.

ESL

3a, Cumulative Adjectives

1. a big brown bear

2. my first new bicycle

3. small round stones

4. an ancient brick fireplace

5. seven large triangular windows

3b, Present and Past Participles

1. Running is energizing.

2. The winter winds here are very drying.

3. She found the doctor's demeanor troubling.

4. Jackie's remarks annoyed me.

5. The new horror movie is frightening.

3c, Adverbs

1. The toddler quickly ate his cereal.

2. There never seems to be enough time.

3. My new neighbor is always in a hurry.

4. I drove fast enough to get to work on time.

5. When we visit New Orleans, we typically eat at Le Meritage Inn.

4a–c, Prepositions 1

1. I went to the movies nearly every week last summer.

2. Put the clean laundry on the bed.

3. When we first moved to Toronto, I missed Hong Kong very much.

4. The best place to look for shoes is in the new shopping mall.

5. After his trip to Somalia, the landscape in New England looked very green to him.

4d–f, Prepositions 2

1. I was not accustomed to wearing my new glasses.

2. My brother's new glasses are for reading.

3. The movie *Precious* was based on the novel *Push* by Sapphire.

4. Four quarters is equal to one dollar.

5. I like to paint as well as to draw.

ESL

5a–b, Omitted Verbs and Subjects

1. My younger brother, who is a professional trumpet player, travels around the world and plays for his fans.

2. Dirk's whole family is very amusing.

3. All my new flowers died after last night's frost.

4. Today's speaker is very dry and boring.

5. The crickets in the trees in my neighborhood sing all day.

ESL

5c, Expletives

1. There are three interstate highways into downtown Atlanta.

2. There are three drawings before the grand prize is given away.

3. Here are all the flowers you ordered from the florist.

4. It is only three days until my birthday.

5. There are many volunteers who are willing to work all night.

ESL

6b, Questions with *Who, Whom,* and *What*

1. Does James want to eat dinner with us tonight?

2. Who created the congressional gridlock?

3. Whom did the instructor choose to go first?

4. Who brings in today's mail?

5. What does the team do?

ESL

6c, Indirect Questions 1

1. How much will the new building and cafeteria cost?

2. Which astronomer first identified black holes?

3. Why are we all here?

4. Which child should he keep an eye on?

5. How does the U.S. Congress differ from the British Parliament?

ESL

6c, Indirect Questions 2

1. She asked if I will be her maid of honor.

2. My brother wasn't sure when I got so smart.

3. I tried to see where my keys went.

4. The committee researched why the cost of education has outpaced inflation in the last ten years.

5. The server asked if I planned on eating on the deck.

ESL

6d, Reported Speech

1. Nino said that he loves zucchini almost as much as he loves peppers.

2. The librarian said, "The new book you want was already checked out."

3. With a grin, Erin stated that Roger has played cello in a faltering but passionate way for years.

4. The president of the company announced, "There will be severe layoffs this summer."

5. The company spokesperson said to wait for the third-quarter results.

ESL

6e, Conditional Sentences

1. If he sees a shooting star, he makes a wish.

2. If you train harder, you can make the team.

3. If I had a better boss, I might have been manager by now.

4. Wherever Fleetwood Mac performed last year, they found big audiences.

5. If you could go anywhere on vacation, where would you go?

XV. GLOSSARY OF USAGE

GLOSSARY

Usage 1

1. We can't leave without Kevin, and he isn't anywhere in the building.

2. The reason Nicholas loved music of all types is he studied music appreciation in college.

3. You should have known every person at the party.

4. What are the effects of smoking?

5. Jason can hardly get his work done because of school.

6. Is your dinner all right?

7. The traffic was so light that we had no problem getting there on time.

GLOSSARY

Usage 2

1. What are the effects of the new spending bill?

   affect: (verb) to change

   effect: (noun) a result; also (verb) to produce

2. It is important that everyone at the meeting remain civil.

   civic: (adj) relating to a city

   civil: (adj) refraining from rudeness

3. Emile can hardly read without going to sleep.

   can't hardly: a double negative and this usage should be avoided

197

4. Regardless of the time it takes to complete the project, you will receive six-thousand dollars.

   irregardless: non-standard for regardless

5. Try to keep Mr. Kessler from going off on a tangent.

   tangible: (adj) something that can be touched

   tangent (go off on a tangent): (verb) to break from a line of thinking; to digress